The Guide to Identity Theft Prevention

By

Johnny R. May, CPP

© 2001 by Johnny R. May. All rights reserved.

No part of this book may be reproduced, stored in a retrieval system, or transmitted by any means, electronic, mechanical, photocopying, recording, or otherwise, without written permission from the author.

ISBN: 0-75964-763-1

This book is printed on acid free paper.

1stBooks – rev. 08/30/01

Acknowledgements

This book is dedicated to my friends, family and colleagues for all their moral support and patience.

A Message from the Publisher

The information presented in this guide is accurate to the best of our knowledge. Every effort has been made to provide the reader with a tool that is useful and accurate in combating the crime of identity theft. The reader is solely responsible for any application of the information presented in this guide. This book was written for informational purposes only. For legal advice consult with an attorney.

Table of Contents

1. Identify Theft: An Overview 1
- What is Identity Theft?...... 2
- Financial Impact...... 3
- Who's at Risk...... 4
- Why Identity Theft Is Attractive to Criminals 6
- Motives of the Identity Thief 6
- Victim Survey Data...... 7
- Identity Theft and the Law...... 9

2. Technology and the Information Age 11
- Internet & Computers...... 12
- Information Brokers 14

3. How Identity Thieves Steal 16
- Mail Theft...... 16
- Fraudulent Changes of Address 18
- Dumpster Diving (aka Trash Napping)...... 18
- Shoulder Surfing 20
- Lost or Stolen Purse/Wallet...... 21
- Insider Access 21
- Internet 23
- Skimmers...... 24
- Pretexting 25

4. Prevention Strategies 27
- Individuals 29
- Police Departments 36
- Employers/Businesses 37
- Creditors 39
- Credit Reporting Agencies 40

5. Your Social Security Number: The Key to It All 42
- What Do Those Numbers Mean? 44
- SSN and Credit Header Information 44
- How the SSN Causes Problems 46
- When Should You Give Out Your Social Security Number? 48

6. False Identification 49

7. If You Become a Victim 52
- Additional Considerations 54
- Your Liability 55
- The Importance of Documentation 57

8. Identity Theft Case Files 60

Appendix A: Credit Bureaus 70
- Requesting Credit Reports and Reporting Fraud 70
- Letter Requesting Removal from Marketing Lists 72

Appendix B: Resources 73
   Organizations 73
   Publications 75
   Identity Theft Websites 77

Appendix C: Check Verification Companies 79

Appendix D: Affidavit of Fraud 80

Appendix E: Letter of Dispute—Template 81

Appendix F: Creditor Dispute Letter—Template 82

Appendix G: State Statutes Relating to Identity Theft 83

Appendix H: The Fair Credit Reporting Act 86

Appendix I: Identity Theft and Assumption Deterrence Act 125

Chapter 1

Identity Theft: An Overview

The crime of identity theft has reached epidemic proportions. While estimates vary, somewhere between 500,000 and 750,000 consumers will become victims of identity theft this year-and the number is growing. According to TransUnion, a credit reporting agency, the total number of inquiries to the company's Fraud Victim Assistance Department skyrocketed from 35,235 in 1992 to 5,222,922 in 1997.[1]

The Federal Trade Commission (FTC), the leading governmental agency addressing the problem of identity theft, has reported a dramatic increase in the incidence of this crime. For example, calls to the FTC identity theft hot line doubled between March and July, 2000-to 850 calls per week. In testimony to a U.S. Senate Judiciary subcommittee, FTC Consumer Protection Bureau Director Jodie Bernstein said, "The fear of identity theft has gripped the public as few consumer issues have."[2]

Why all the fear? Most likely it's because a target of identity theft usually doesn't know he has become a victim until he has a credit application denied or receives a phone call from a collection agency seeking payment. It is a very troubling prospect!

What is Identity Theft?

Identity theft occurs when someone uses the identifying information of another person-name, social security number, mother's maiden name, etc.-to commit fraud or engage in other unlawful activities.[3] While numerous variations of the crime exist, an identity thief can fraudulently use personal identifying information to, among other things:

- open new credit card accounts;
- take over existing credit card accounts;
- apply for loans;
- rent apartments;
- establish services with utility companies;
- write fraudulent checks using another person's name and account number;
- steal and transfer money from existing bank accounts;
- file bankruptcy; and
- obtain employment using the victim's name.

The Guide to Identity Theft Prevention

Ironically, the dollar losses aren't the greatest concern for most victims. For example, Federal law limits a consumer's liability for credit card fraud to $50 per account, and some credit card companies even have zero liability policies.

The real problem for most victims, as you'll soon find out, is straightening out a damaged credit history.

Financial Impact

Identity theft is difficult to track because it can range from a simple unauthorized use of a credit card to complete takeover of a person's identity. But no one doubts that the financial hit is substantial-and growing rapidly. In 1998, the U.S. General Accounting Office reported on losses stemming from identity theft. The Secret Service, for example, investigated $442 million in identity theft losses in 1995; in 1997, that figure rose to $745 million. That same year, Mastercard told the GAO it had lost $407 million because of fraud-with 96 percent of that due to identity theft.[4]

Identity theft also involves indirect costs. All of us pay when companies increase their prices to recover losses due to identity theft.

Who's at Risk

When confronted with the topic of identity theft, a common response is "it will never happen to me." But some experts say it's no longer a matter of *whether* you will become a victim of identity theft, but *when*.

A common misconception is that only the wealthy or creditworthy are targeted by identity thieves. However, *no one is immune*. Anyone with a social security number is at risk. Identity theft is a crime of opportunity. Identity thieves will impersonate anyone whose information they can obtain. Even if it's from an obituary!

Here is just one example. A North Dakota man received a call from his bank wanting to know why he had applied for a loan to buy a new pickup when he had just taken one out for a new vehicle. Then he received a call from another bank asking for payment on bounced checks totaling almost $9,000. The real shock came when he went to renew his drivers license in the same town where he grew up. The clerk looked at the man, then at the records, and told the man that he was not who he said he was. The computer spit out a license with the victim's name and another man's photo on it. The thief, a veteran con artist, had obtained a copy of the victim's birth certificate for $10 from

The Guide to Identity Theft Prevention

a gullible state employee. How had the con man picked out his victim? From an obituary for the victim's deceased brother.[5]

Popular targets of identity thieves are people with common names, as well as mothers, daughters, juniors and seniors with the same name. "Identity thieves exploit the inherent confusion over such names," said David Szwak, a Louisiana attorney who has filed more than 100 lawsuits on behalf of identity theft victims.[6]

According to the U.S. Census Bureau, here are the most common names in the United States:

- <u>Family Names:</u> Smith, Johnson, Williams, Jones, Brown, Davis, Miller, Wilson, Moore, Taylor
- <u>Males</u>: James, John, Robert, Michael, William, David, Richard, Charles, Joseph, Thomas
- <u>Females</u>: Mary, Patricia, Linda, Barbara, Elizabeth, Jennifer, Maria, Susan, Margaret, Dorothy

The bottom line is that the more common your name, the more at risk you are.

Why Identity Theft Is Attractive to Criminals

Criminals are attracted to the low risk and high rewards that identity theft provides. First of all, the law treats identity theft as a crime against property, and in general the penalties for property crimes are less severe than for crimes against a person. Most career criminals know this. They also know that the majority of law enforcement attention goes to high profile crimes such as homicide, rape and robbery.

To make matters worse, police departments often lack the resources to properly investigate identity crimes. The thieves are very seldom apprehended. Even when brought to justice, they usually receive lenient sentences.

Motives of the Identity Thief

Identity thieves steal for various reasons. There are three main motives:

Financial gain: This is the most common reason. The goal of identity thieves is to drain all bank and credit card accounts and then move on to the next victim.

Revenge: Their main goal is to avenge perceived mistreatment, or to ruin the victim's

The Guide to Identity Theft Prevention

credit history and reputation. This may be accomplished by creating a criminal record or derogatory credit history using the victim's name.

Fresh start: By assuming someone else's identity, the identity thief can cover up a criminal record or a poor credit or employment history and lead a "normal" life. There are actually books for sale that teach how to use counterfeiting and other techniques to establish a new identity-an identity with good credit.

Sometimes identity thieves will steal for other reasons as well. For example, an expectant mother admitted herself into a Florida hospital for the delivery of her baby. But she wasn't who she said she was. She had stolen a former neighbor's identity and insurance information. The victim, who had moved to Texas, received phone calls from the hospital demanding payment. She figured out what had happened and contacted the police.

Victim Survey Data

A survey of 66 identity theft victims was conducted by the California Public Interest Group (CALPIRG) and the Privacy Rights Clearinghouse. The survey, which explored the specific problems encountered by victims of identity theft, revealed the following:

- The average victim learned about identity theft 14 months after it occurred.
- More than half (55%) of the victims considered their cases unsolved at the time of the survey, with their cases having been open an average of 44 months.
- Victims spent an average of 175 hours actively trying to clear their names.
- The average total fraudulent charges made on new and existing accounts of survey respondents was $18,000.
- Three-quarters of victims felt the police had been unhelpful, finding that officers issued police reports less than 75 percent of the time and assigned a detective to the case less than half the time.
- Respondents found out about identity theft in one of two ways: they were denied credit or a loan because of a negative credit report stemming from fraudulent accounts, or a creditor or debt collection agency contacted them about payment.[7]

In fairness to the police, it should be noted that, until 1998, there were almost no statutes making identity theft a crime or specifying police response.

Also, there was little in the way of financial support for departments to deal effectively with this issue. However, that is changing-rapidly-and both laws and resources have been brought to bear in many states. Many police departments now have special task forces to deal with crimes of identity.

Identity Theft and the Law

Until recently, neither the federal government nor most states had laws addressing the crime of identity theft. However, that has changed. Currently, more than three quarters of the states have passed laws relating to this crime. A listing of current state statutes as of this writing is included in Appendix G of this book.

Meanwhile, at the federal level, Congress passed the Identity Theft and Assumption Deterrence Act of 1998. This law made it a federal crime when anyone.

knowingly transfers or uses, without lawful authority, a means of identification of another person with the intent to commit, or to aid or abet, any unlawful activity that constitutes a violation of federal law, or that constitutes a felony under any applicable state or local law.[8]

Violations of the Act are investigated by federal investigative agencies such as the U.S. Secret Service, the FBI, and the U.S. Postal Inspection Service, and prosecuted by the Department of Justice. See Appendix I for more information about the Identity Theft Assumption and Deterrence Act.

Chapter 2

Technology and the Information Age

The adage "information is power" holds true in today's high tech computer age. The computerization of personal information has created a whole new type of criminal. Records and information, which once took days or weeks to obtain, can now be gathered in a matter of minutes or hours using a home computer. Today, if a person has money and desire, there's almost nothing he or she can't find out about you.

For example, access to drivers license information has traditionally been restricted to law enforcement officials. But now some states allow the purchase of such information over the Internet. South Carolina and Florida officials sold millions of digital photos of drivers licenses to private companies. As you might expect, this raised serious questions about personal privacy. After numerous consumer complaints, both states placed greater restrictions on the sale of digital photographs.[9] However, it is nevertheless becoming more common for consumers and companies to seek and gain access to this information.

Internet & Computers

Computers make it possible for anyone to gather mass amounts of personal information about each and every one of us. Much of this information is available for a price on the Internet.

In a recent case, a California woman downloaded credit reports from the same websites used by landlords to conduct background checks on prospective tenants. Some sites sent her the reports after nothing more than a mouse click promise that she would use the information legally. At the time of her arrest, the woman had financial data on more than 300 people.[10]

A curious news correspondent recently decided to see just how easy it is to get supposedly confidential financial records from the credit checking sites currently being abused by identity thieves. It took him only two minutes and $14.95 to access his spouse's credit report.[11]

The Internet has done two things. First, it makes public records quickly accessible to anyone who wants them. Even though most of this information has always been a matter of public record, how to access it has not been common knowledge. Now anyone with a computer and Internet access can obtain it. The second thing the Internet has done is allow identity thieves to work anonymously from anywhere in the world. In the past, a criminal would have to visit a bank or lending institution to apply for an account, increasing the risk of being captured. However, with instant credit on the Internet, a criminal is highly unlikely to be captured, while the prospective reward for the thief has increased.[12]

Today, an identity thief armed with a social security number and other personal information can apply for credit cards over the Internet with little scrutiny from card issuers. Shopping on the Internet is also easy because the credit transactions are not made face to face. By using a credit card a few times and paying monthly balances, the identity thief can quickly establish what appears to be a solid credit history-and gain the credibility to apply for high dollar value items such as cars.

"Hacking" is also becoming more common as a means to commit identity theft. This is where a computer user slips by electronic security and password barriers to gain access to a company's computer server, or sometimes the server of an Internet service provider (ISP). Then they steal names, addresses, credit card numbers and other information. In one case, individuals hacked into an ISP computer server and stole the records for 10,000 customers! Then they sent a message to the ISP offering to return the stolen data for $30,000. In the end, the hackers were apprehended and charged with extortion-but only after doing considerable damage.[13]

Phony websites have also been used to commit identity theft. For example, one cyber-criminal decided to impersonate the FBI in order to obtain social security numbers and other personal information.. He put together a fake website complete with FBI logo. It looked like the real thing-it even featured an official-looking "Freedom of Information Act" request form. Many citizens like to request information from the government, and so the presence of such a request form on the website contributed to the perception of its authenticity. Visitors to the website unhesitatingly furnished the information requested-and supplied their credit card numbers to pay the $10 application fee. Needless to say, no one ever got what they paid for-but they did get plenty of trouble in the form of undoing the damages done to their credit records.[14]

Information Brokers

Information brokers have been around for decades, furnishing information to attorneys, private investigators and other licensed professionals. However, a new breed of information broker has emerged in recent years-the

The Guide to Identity Theft Prevention

kind that sells personal information to anyone requesting it via the Internet. Driven by greed, some information brokers are careless when they receive an order. They fail to verify the identity of the requestor and do little, if any, probing into the intended use of the information.

A recent and gruesome example will illustrate how serious this problem can be. An online information broker was recently sued by the parents of a young woman slain by an Internet stalker. The suit alleges that for $109, the broker had sold personal information that led the killer to the victim's place of employment. He then ambushed her as she got into her car after leaving work.

Chapter 3

How Identity Thieves Steal

It has often been said that the best offense is a good defense. You must understand the identity thief's mode of operation if you are to successfully defend against an attack.

Listed below are some of the most common techniques used by criminals to steal identities.

Mail Theft

A red flag on a mailbox is an open invitation to identity thieves. If a person leaves outgoing bills in the mailbox for the postal carrier to pick up, a thief can use the information to obtain credit in the victim's name. What's so alarming is that it takes only one stolen item-an outgoing bill, an incoming bank account statement-and the identity thief has all the information he or she needs to cause havoc. According to Corporal Albert Jeffcoat, an officer with the Savannah, Georgia Police Department and representative of the Coastal Empire Alliance Against Fraud, a single fraudulent check can victimize up to seven businesses and individuals.[15]

The Guide to Identity Theft Prevention

A common method of operation employs a process known as check washing. Identity thieves erase the ink on a check using common household cleaning products such as acetone or bleach. Then they rewrite the checks to themselves, often increasing the amount payable by hundreds or thousands of dollars. A thief can steal a check in the morning when the victim leaves for work, and cash it by that afternoon. Bank and credit card statements, pre-approved credit card offers, telephone calling cards, and drivers license numbers all make attractive targets for the mail thief.

Mail carriers have also been victimized. In Los Angeles, gang members discovered that carriers use "arrow keys" to open many of the boxes on their routes-from personal boxes to huge drop-off centers. They began terrorizing the carriers, holding them up at knife and gunpoint, demanding keys and the mail. Ultimately, a cadre of members from the Crips gang extorted 26 of the arrow keys. Over a three-year period, they are believed to have stolen letters and parcels in the tens of thousands. In one apartment, authorities found that the gang had stashed $280,000 worth of washed and counterfeit checks. The case prompted an expensive re-keying of the mailboxes so the keys wouldn't work anymore.[16]

Fraudulent Changes of Address

In this scenario, the criminal fills out a change of address form at the post office so that the victim's mail is redirected to the thief's address or mail drop. The thief then obtains bank and credit card or other mail containing the information necessary to take over the victim's identity. Some identity theft rings will even rent inexpensive apartments specifically for the purpose of receiving this mail. Sometimes they will rent the apartment in the name of the victim using a piece of fake identification obtained in the victim's name.[17]

Fortunately, authorities are taking some actions to discourage this activity. For example, identity thieves generally won't use mail forwarding or commercial mailboxes because credit bureau alert programs will identify these addresses. And the Postal Service recently implemented changes to discourage fraudulent changes of address.

Dumpster Diving (aka Trash Napping)

One man's trash is another man's treasure!

Some identity thieves love trash-especially if it is from upscale neighborhoods or business establishments. With a quick call to the sanitation

The Guide to Identity Theft Prevention

company, thieves can learn the day and time of garbage pick-up for the targeted area. Then they usually go in early in the morning before sunrise or late at night, using darkness to conceal their identity. After finding a secluded area to go through their "haul," the thieves look for any item that may contain personal identifiers-bank or credit card statements, pre-approved credit card offers, etc.

Business dumpsters are particularly attractive. Criminals know that these receptacles can contain treasure troves of information about business and customer accounts. Many of these "dumpster divers" disguise themselves as homeless people. Also, a lot of organized identity theft ringleaders hire drug addicts and alcoholics to collect items from the trash.[18] Another common method of "trash napping" is employed by cleaning crews. They use their access to office and industrial property to secure a steady stream of business trash.

Businesses most often targeted by trash nappers and dumpster divers include:

* Banks   * Restaurants
* Hotels   * Service Stations
* Travel Agencies   * Pharmacies
* Hospitals   * Airline Ticket Offices

One of the hottest items that divers search for these days is checks-even invalid ones. In one case, a thief went on a spending spree after finding checks from a closed out account in the trash. It was a case of simple forgery using supposedly worthless checks. Canceled checks are also a prize-the thieves "wash" the checks using a chemical process that removes the ink from the paper. Or, using an off-the-shelf software package available at most office supply stores, they can scan the canceled check and use computer graphics to clean it up and make it look like new.

<u>You don't need the physical check</u>, however, to be an identity thief. Just the account number on the check will suffice. One man, operating out of a California hotel, paid dozens of dumpster divers to sort through trash in search of checking account numbers.[19] After collecting the valid numbers, the thief used his laptop computer to produce checks with altered names. And as many law enforcement officials will attest, such checks are not difficult to pass off at stores.

Shoulder Surfing

Anytime you use an ATM or calling card in a public place you put yourself at risk. Shoulder surfers are criminals who lurk around ATM machines and payphones in high traffic areas such as airports, hotels and shopping centers. They observe from afar, sometimes using binoculars or camcorders, hoping to catch a glimpse of your personal identification number (PIN) or calling card number. If they get your calling card number, they can sell it on the street. Buyers can use your calling card to make long distance calls for free. With ATM cards, thieves watch and learn the individual's card number and PIN number. Later, they will steal the card or make their own and go back to the ATM to withdraw cash.

Lost or Stolen Purse/Wallet

Old-fashioned pick-pocketing is still a lucrative trade. Nowadays, however, cash is often the last thing that motivates the criminal. A lost or stolen wallet or purse provides the identity thief with a wealth of personal information which he may use to obtain credit or commit crimes in the victim's name.

Insider Access

An employee of a business may wrongfully retrieve personal identification that the business has collected for legitimate reasons. The employee then may sell the information, or use it to obtain credit in the victim's name. Recently, more sophisticated schemes are gaining popularity. One such method is securing entry-level employment with a financial institution or other company. This may provide the identity thief access to credit reports or other personal data, for exploitation or use by identity theft rings.[20] This happened at General Motors Corporation, where a ring of identity thieves targeted a group of high-ranking executives. A temporary employee at the company's world headquarters obtained personal information about the executives and then sold it. The information, including social security numbers and birth dates, was used to get credit cards. The police estimated that about $100,000 was charged to the cards.[21]

Surprisingly enough, a lot of times the identity thief is someone from the victim's inner circle-a roommate, relative, client, health caregiver, etc.- who has easy access to the victim's residence and personal records. In one case, the adult daughter of a Michigan couple obtained credit cards in their name and ran up debts of more than $10,000. She paid the interest fees so as not to alert her parents of her use of the cards, but was not able to keep up with the payments. The credit card companies were able to hold the parents accountable for the bills, given that the debtor was their daughter.

Internet

Like almost everyone else, criminals are becoming "high tech."

Anyone, including criminals, can purchase personal information via the Internet and misuse it to obtain credit in the victim's name. Much of this information is available from credit bureaus. That is because there has been little in the way of statutory restriction (at least so far) on the release or sale of non-credit related consumer information. Such information, commonly referred to as "credit header" information, is located in the top portion of a credit report and typically consists of an individual's name, name variations, date of birth, social security number and current as well as previous addresses.[22] Although credit header information is generated as part of the credit reporting process, the Federal Trade Commission has determined that it is not part of the credit history and therefore is not regulated under the Fair Credit Reporting Act. Thus, you should be aware that no legitimate reason is required to obtain header reports-including *your* header reports-which can be purchased on the Internet for a nominal fee.

Another target of high-tech identity thieves is personal web pages. Many are loaded with information such as full names, birth dates, addresses, occupations, degrees and phone numbers. Genealogy fans like to research family trees. They often place details online such as a mother's maiden name. However, such information is commonly used as a password for credit cards and bank accounts. Therefore, individuals who put such information on their personal or genealogical web pages are increasingly at risk for identity theft.

Skimmers

Shoppers beware. The advent of easy-to-use skimmers and the Internet has made it easy for criminals to victimize businesses that accept credit cards and ATM debit cards. A skimmer is a device that is smaller than a deck of cards which can read the magnetized strips on bank or credit cards the same way credit card scanners and ATM machines read card information. They can capture and retain information from the cards, including account numbers, balances and verification codes.

One recent Christmas, at Bloomingdale's in New York City, an independent vendor in the store's sunglasses department was arrested after she swiped a customer's credit card through a skimmer and transferred its information to a palm-held data organizer.[23] These popular devices can each store thousands of credit card numbers, which can then be printed on bogus cards or e-mailed for use anywhere in the world.

Restaurants are also a place to be on guard. Last year, waiters at two New York restaurants used card skimmers to swipe customer credit cards. In one case, 15 stolen card numbers added up to a $250,000 shopping spree. Fortunately, the waiters were caught. They were fired and prosecuted.

Pretexting

Sometimes, identity thieves will try to trick others into revealing personal information. One way they do this is by "pretexting," or calling under false pretenses such as by contacting banks and posing as the account holder. In other cases, the identity thief may contact the victim directly. For example, in one scheme criminals played on consumer fears about the Y2k computer bug. In this scam, the caller pretended to represent the victim's bank. He either asked the victim to supply certain information about the account, or, in another variation, persuaded the victim to transfer money to a special account in order to ensure the bank could comply with Y2k requirements.[24] Pretexting appears to be gaining popularity in response to the booming market for comprehensive personal information relating to consumers.[25]

Chapter 4

Prevention Strategies

As stated in Chapter 1, the crime of identity theft has reached epidemic proportions. It has become so bad that society has resorted to innovative approaches to combating this crime.

For example, the Los Angeles County Sheriff's Department was one of the first law enforcement agencies in the country to create a specialized unit dealing with identity theft. The unit focuses on several areas including department-wide training and public education. The unit coordinates its efforts with public and private agencies such as the California Department of Motor Vehicles, credit card companies and banks. The unit also has developed a guidebook for victims with numbers to call for information and help, as well as guides for field deputies.[26] Police agencies in South Carolina and elsewhere have formed a coalition to respond to the alarming increase in identity theft and educate financial institutions, businesses and the public about this crime.[27]

Meanwhile, at least one insurance company, the Travelers Property Casualty Corporation, now offers consumers insurance protection for expenses associated with the growing crime of identity theft. The coverage, called Identity Theft Fraud Expense coverage, can be added to a homeowner, condominium or renter policy for an additional premium of $25 per year and provides $15,000 coverage with $100 deductible. The coverage reimburses the policyholder for expenses incurred as a result of efforts to clear her name after becoming a victim of identity theft. Expenses covered include legal expenses, loan re-application fees, telephone and certified mailing charges, notary expenses, and lost wages.[28]

How much does it cost to reinstate your good name? According to a May 2000 survey by the Privacy Rights Clearinghouse and the California Public Interest Research Group (CALPIRG), victims reported spending anywhere from $30 to $2000 each on costs related to their identity theft, not including lawyer fees. The average loss was $808.[29]

While no one can guarantee you will not become a victim of identity theft, you can greatly minimize the chances of becoming a victim by implementing the safeguards mentioned below:

The Guide to Identity Theft Prevention
Individuals

1. Be extremely cautious when handling and disclosing the following information: social security number, mother's maiden name, date of birth, past addresses, drivers license number, and, of course, bank and credit account numbers.

2. Invest in a personal shredder. This is your first line of defense. Shred bank and credit card statements, canceled checks, pre-approved credit card offers, etc. before disposal. A cross cut shredder offers added security because it makes it harder to reconstruct the document.

3. Place garbage out on the morning of pickup rather than the night before. This gives dumpster divers less opportunity to go through your garbage.

4. Consider listing only your name and phone number in the telephone book or get an unlisted and unpublished number. If you do have a personal or business listing, avoid the use of titles such as "Dr." or "Attorney", or any other signs announcing you're affluent.

5. Be aware of other directories in which you may be listed. In addition to the telephone directory (see previous item), criminals have been known to find victims in "Who's Who" and other publications.

6. Install a residential mailbox with a locking mechanism or purchase a door with a mail slot.

7. Don't leave outgoing checks or paid bills in your residential mailbox. Take your mail to the post office or drop it in a U.S. Postal Service mailbox. Also, consider paying bills electronically; a lot of financial institutions now offer this option.

8. Opt out of pre-approved credit card offers by calling (888) 5OPTOUT, or (888) 567-8688. Your request covers all three major credit bureaus (Experian, TransUnion and Equifax).

9. When you order new checks, do not have them sent to your residence. Pick them up at the bank instead. Or, have them delivered to you by registered mail-so you have to sign for them personally.

The Guide to Identity Theft Prevention

10. Call your credit card company if your card has expired and you have not yet received a replacement.

11. Minimize the amount of information you carry in your wallet or purse. This can be accomplished by limiting the number of credit cards you carry with you. Also, don't carry your social security card.

12. To avoid pickpockets, men should carry wallets in a front pants pocket or a buttoned or zippered back pocket. Another idea is to place a rubber band around the wallet so it will rub against the cloth, alerting the potential victim a crime is in progress.

13. For women, a purse with a zippered compartment and a flap over the outside works best; carry the purse on your side, with the flap against your body. Avoid drawstring purses.

14. Scrutinize monthly billing statements. Open bills promptly and check your accounts monthly. Look for charges you don't recognize and report them immediately. Report late statements. Save receipts to compare with your billing statements.

15. Keep your eyes on your credit card during all transactions (e.g., in restaurants), and get it back as soon as possible.

16. Keep a record of all your credit card account numbers, expiration dates, and the telephone number and address of each creditor. Store it in a secure place.

17. Be cautious of "shoulder surfers". This crime most often occurs with calling cards. Always shield your calling card number by placing your hand over the telephone keypad or look for a phone with a card swipe.

18. Order a copy of your credit report at least 1-2 times per year from each of the three major credit bureaus (Experian, TransUnion, and Equifax). Look for address changes and fraudulent accounts. Check for accuracy. Do this on your birthday to help you remember to do it at least once per year.

19. Order credit reports for your children as well. It is easy to overlook the possibility of fraud involving your child's social security number.

20. Don't voluntarily give out personal information such as credit card numbers or social security

The Guide to Identity Theft Prevention

numbers over the phone unless you initiated the phone call. Ask for a call back number and match it against the telephone book or directory assistance. Check with the Better Business Bureau or other agencies to determine the legitimacy of the business.

21. Ask your creditors to include a security password on your accounts. Stay away from using a mother's maiden name or your social security number. While you won't make a lot of points with your creditors, you will provide yourself with an added blanket of security.

22. Cancel credit cards that you seldom use. The more open accounts you have, the more vulnerable you are.

23. Limit the amount of information you place on your Internet homepage, and on websites detailing family genealogy.

24. Limit the personal information on your checks. Don't pre-print your social security number, telephone number, or driver's license number on your checks. Disclose it only when absolutely required. If a merchant asks you for your telephone number or driver's license number, you may decide to add it at that time.

Johnny R. May

A retailer should have no need for your social security number.

25. Ask your employer and others not to use your social security number as an identifier; use an alternative number if possible.

26. Do not allow sales clerks to copy your credit card numbers onto checks for additional information. It's against the law in many states, and major credit card companies prohibit merchants from charging a customer's credit card account to cover a bad check. Be aware, however, that unless you are in one of the states where this act is illegal, the merchant can refuse to make the sale if you refuse to furnish the requested information.

27. Never write down personal identifications numbers (PINs) or passwords; memorize them. Do not use your social security number or any easy-to-guess words or number sequences such as birth dates.

28. When ordering online, it is generally preferable to use a credit card instead of a debit card, because of the immediacy with which a debit card will give a thief access to the cash in your bank account. However, Federal law does

The Guide to Identity Theft Prevention

protect both credit and debit card users. If you notify your bank or card issuer immediately upon discovering questionable charges to your account, your liability is usually limited to $50 per card. Please read your account terms or contact your bank or card issuer to be sure of your rights.

29. Before purchasing online, find out if the site has a secure server. Secure pages begin with "https" instead of "http". A picture of a lock in the locked position should appear on the browser window.

30. You can purchase services which alert you when there are irregularities in your accounts. Such services include Experian Fraudshield and ID Guard.

Police Departments

1. Create identity theft or white collar crime units to investigate identity theft cases and educate the public about identity theft. Work with banks, credit card companies and other public and private agencies.

2. Promote department-wide training on identity theft. Educate officers on identity theft and various methods used by identity thieves to steal.

3. Increase patrols in residential areas on garbage collection days.

4. Offer to have crime prevention officers conduct security surveys of businesses to identify vulnerabilities (such as information systems and trash disposal) and make recommendations to better protect the personal information of employees and customers.

5. Provide members of the community with pamphlets or brochures about identity theft. Crime prevention officers can also conduct training seminars on the topic.

The Guide to Identity Theft Prevention

6. Provide public access to your crime prevention video library, or encourage the public library to stock relevant publications and audiovisual programs. Work with local media to make sure people know what's available.

Employers/Businesses

1. Properly dispose of personal information and other sensitive material. This could be accomplished by shredding documents. Do not allow intact documents to be thrown in dumpsters.

2. Conduct background checks on all individuals with access to personal and/or sensitive information, including cleaning and temporary service personnel.

3. Limit the number of temporary agencies your company uses. If possible, maintain the services of one trusted firm.

4. Be sure your cleaning service is licensed and bonded. Do the same with any other contractors that are granted access to your premises.

5. Develop guidelines to safeguard sensitive information; the guidelines should address issues such as practices for handling such information responsibly.

6. Train staff on information security issues and include information on the topic in new employee orientations. Educate them on why certain information needs protection and procedures on how to protect it.

7. Security awareness could also be increased through the use of posters, newsletters, brochures, e-mails and other promotion vehicles that address proper information handling practices.

8. Contact your local police department and request a security survey of your facility. Many departments will provide this service free of charge.

9. Limit the use of the Social security number (SSN) in the workplace. Don't use the number on items such as employee identification badges, time cards or paychecks for the whole world to see. Use alternative numbers.

10. Control access to personal information and limit it to those employees who have a legitimate reason for access.

11. Secure employees' personal information in a locked file cabinet or other secure area. Sensitive files stored on the computer should be password protected and encrypted.

12. Implement and enforce password security procedures for all computer users. Passwords should be changed on a regularly scheduled basis.

Creditors

1. Issue credit cards with a photo of the cardholder printed on them to prevent fraudulent use.

2. Assist customers in selecting security passwords for accounts; discourage the use of mother's maiden name or social security number.

3. Notify consumers if they receive a change of address request for additional cards at an address other than that on record.

4. Use a software system that monitors spending patterns. Such a system detects irregular increases in your customers' spending habits and sends up red flags.

5. Truncate account numbers printed on transaction slips at point-of-sales. This measure limits access to full account numbers by concealing some of the numbers.

6. Ask for supplemental identification verification such as a utility or phone bill when credit cards are granted using pre-approved credit card offers.

Credit Reporting Agencies

1. Provide consumers with one free credit report from each of the three major credit bureaus per year, upon request, in all states.

2. Contact the customer whenever an inquiry is made into his/her credit record. Make the contact at the original address of record.

3. Place fraud alerts on the front page of credit reports in a highly visible location. Impose fines and punishment for establishments that

The Guide to Identity Theft Prevention

are negligent and grant credit after fraud alerts have been implemented.

4. Inform credit issuers of fraud even if they only request the credit score.

5. Stop selling the consumer's personal information without his/her consent. Offer initial opt-out opportunities.

Chapter 5

Your Social Security Number: The Key to It All

When the social security number was created in 1935, Americans were promised their numbers would not be used as national identification numbers and would only be used to monitor contributions to the federal pension system. In fact, social security cards used to be marked "not for identification purposes." Today, the social security number has become ubiquitous. Employers display social security numbers on employee name badges, parking permits and personnel records. College professors post grades by social security numbers in an attempt to protect student privacy. (What an irony, since this number is the very key to unlocking the door to private information!)

Listed below are just a few of the many other places social security numbers are posted or displayed:

Military ID cards
Medicare cards
College ID cards
Banking and savings account statements
College and alumni records
Insurance records
Tax returns
Credit bureau header reports

The list goes on and on.

The truth is, anyone can steal your identity and ruin your credit rating and reputation. All they need is your social security number. Then why is this number so readily available? The answer is: for convenience. Businesses know that phone numbers, addresses and names change, but social security numbers for the most part do not.

Until Internet use became commonplace, the concern about social security numbers and threats to personal privacy remained relatively minimal. The P-Trak controversy in 1996 helped to change that, by demonstrating that personal identifiers, such as social security numbers, were being sold through on-line services. Created by Lexis-Nexis, this on-line service allowed individuals to enter a name and receive the corresponding social security number. The program created such an outcry that the company suspended search capability of the program within two weeks of its introduction.

What Do Those Numbers Mean?

Every social security number has nine digits. The first three digits represent the state where the card was issued. The middle two digits have no special significance but merely serve to break the numbers into blocks of convenient size. The last four digits of a social security number represent a straight numerical progression of assigned numbers. These last four digits are commonly used by banks and credit card companies to enable customers to access account information over the phone. So it's really the last four digits that identify an individual.[30]

SSN and Credit Header Information

One of the most common sources for obtaining social security numbers is credit reports. Up until the late 1980's the Fair Credit Reporting Act required a business to have a permissible purpose to gain access to a consumer's credit report. However, the Federal Trade Commission later removed the privacy protection from all parts of the credit report except for actual credit history. Now credit header information can be sold to anyone who wants to purchase it.

What is the credit header? It's the identifying information that accompanies a consumer's credit reports. It consists of name, name variations, addresses, former addresses, telephone numbers, date of birth and social security number. The credit header data are sold separately from the credit history and are widely used by private investigators, skip tracers, attorneys, information brokers and other groups who specialize in locating individuals-including those whose purpose is identity theft.

Legislation has been proposed to limit the use of credit header information. U.S. Senator Diane Feinstein, D-Calif., introduced a bill that would limit the use of social security numbers by prohibiting commercial acquisition, distribution and use of the numbers without permission. Specifically, it would prevent credit card companies and other such agencies from selling header information to other companies. It would also prevent the Department of Motor Vehicles from giving out personal information for surveys or solicitors.

How the SSN Causes Problems

In the wrong hands, the social security number can wreak havoc. For example, a desk clerk at the University of Florida spent over $100,000 using credit cards he acquired using student social security numbers. By the time the clerk was caught, he had used the stolen identities to purchase stereos, computer printers, televisions, a riding lawnmower and a washing machine.

In 1967, the military made the decision to use the social security number as a military serial number. Access to this information enabled a prisoner at a federal facility in Missouri to turn his assignment to a clothing room into a lucrative scam. His job was to sort out army fatigues from Fort Leonard Wood. As a longtime veteran of tax fraud, it didn't take him long to figure out that the discarded uniforms delivered to his station were a potential gold mine: On each piece of clothing was a soldier's name and social security number.

The identity thief requested blank tax forms by mail and filed phony tax returns and requests for refunds, using the names and social security numbers on the different forms. This generated more than 200 refund checks mailed to addresses selected by the criminal. The IRS discovered the fraud and was able to stop many of the refund checks. However, the Army continued for some time to send old uniforms to the federal detention facility, with social security numbers and names on each piece.[31]

In a separate incident, a retired air force colonel and his wife became the victims of identity theft. It all started in 1997, when they were about to move from Maryland to South Carolina to build a retirement home. Then one day they received a call demanding payment on a Jeep Cherokee. The only problem was the couple didn't own a Jeep Cherokee. They later found out someone 1500 miles away in Texas had used the colonel's social security number and good credit to purchase the jeep. How could this have happened? Probably because on the military bases where they had served, almost every single transaction record had their social security numbers on it. For the air force couple, it didn't stop with one Jeep Cherokee. Their credit report revealed that, in all, five cars had been bought using their social security numbers, including another Jeep Cherokee, a Ford Ranger pickup truck, a 1988 Ford Bronco and a 1995 Plymouth Neon. In all, a total of 33 separate fraudulent accounts were opened in their names, totaling $113,000.[32]

Johnny R. May

When Should You Give Out Your Social Security Number?

There are restrictions on government agencies asking for your social security number. The Privacy Act of 1974 requires all government agencies that use your social security number-federal, state and local-to provide you with a disclosure statement. The statement tells whether you're required to provide your social security number or whether it's optional, how the social security number will be used, and what will happen if you refuse to provide it. If you are asked to give the number to a government agency and no disclosure statement is included on the form, complain and cite the Privacy Act.[33]

When dealing with private organizations, you are not compelled by law to disclose your social security number. You may choose not to supply your social security number, but by the same token, a private organization may refuse you its goods or services. Keep in mind that employers are required by the IRS to get the social security number of the people they employ.

Banks and various others are also required by the IRS to report the social security number of account holders to whom they pay interest.

Chapter 6

False Identification

The major weapon in the identity thief's arsenal is false identification. Today's identity thieves are not armed with knives or guns, but high tech desktop publishing equipment such as computers and color laser printers. Most types of identity theft involve false identification at some point or another. The following documents are commonly counterfeited or fraudulently obtained:

- social security cards
- state drivers licenses
- passports/visas
- voter registrations

In San Francisco, an identity theft ring specializing in mail theft used a variety of computers and color printers to generate phony identifications from the documents they had stolen. The ring was ultimately traced and caught after police determined that the counterfeiting was being done with a specialized color printer, which required a particular cartridge available only in certain computer supply stores.[34] Hundreds of fraudulent drivers licenses, replicas of credit and ATM cards, and numerous fake checks were confiscated by the police. Thousands of dollars worth of equipment, including digital cameras, hologram imprinting devices, and dozens of PCs, printers and scanners were seized.

One major problem is that many merchants are unable to tell the difference between authentic and false identification. It's even more confusing when merchants are presented with out-of-state checks and identification cards with which they are not familiar.

An excellent resource for these businesses is <u>The Id Checking Guide</u>. This guide has examples of valid drivers licenses from all 50 states, the Canadian provinces, Puerto Rico and Mexico. It includes full-color, actual-size photographs of current, former and "under 21" versions of each license and state ID card. Because the guide is produced in cooperation with several jurisdictions, it lists the security features, license number format, terms of license, and potential variations between issuing bodies.[35]

The Guide to Identity Theft Prevention

The ID Checking Guide is published by :

The Drivers License Guide Company
PO Box 5305, Dept 98
Redwood City, CA 94063
www.idcheckingguide.com

There are two other books worth mentioning for security or law enforcement professionals who are interested in finding out how criminals go about creating new identities. They are:

The Modern Identity Changer: How to Create a New Identity for Privacy and Personal Freedom by Sheldon Charrett (Boulder, CO: Paladin Press, 1997/ ISBN: 0-87364-946-x)

Identity, Privacy, and Personal Freedom: Big Brother vs. the New Resistance by Sheldon Charrett (Boulder, CO: Paladin Press, 1999/ ISBN: 1-58160-042-9)

See Appendix B for additional sources of information on identity theft.

Chapter 7

If You Become a Victim

How do you know you've become a victim of identity theft? Some red flags or indicators might include the following:

- You are denied credit
- A new or renewed credit card never arrives in the mail
- You start receiving calls from creditors about debts you have no knowledge of
- You discover unauthorized purchases on your billing statements

If someone has stolen your identity, the Federal Trade Commission recommends that you take three actions immediately:[36]

1. Contact the fraud departments of each of the three major credit bureaus. Tell them to flag your file with a fraud alert including a statement that creditors should call you for permission before they open any new accounts in your name. Also request a copy of your credit report and check it

The Guide to Identity Theft Prevention

for accuracy. Ask the credit bureaus to remove the fraudulent information.

To Report Fraud

Equifax (www.equifax.com)   (800) 525-6285

Experian (www.experian.com) (888) 397-3742

Trans Union (www.tuc.com)   (800) 680-7289

2. Contact your creditors about any accounts that have been tampered with or opened fraudulently. Ask to speak with someone in the security or fraud department, and *follow up in writing*. Following up with a letter is one of the procedures spelled out in the Fair Credit Billing Act for resolving errors on credit card billing statements, including charges or electronic fund transfers that you have not made.

3. File a police report with the local police where the identity theft took place. Get a copy of the report in case the bank, credit card company or other parties need proof of the crime later on. Insist that you be given a complaint number.

Additional Considerations

Right now, when you report identity theft to your creditors, each one may require you to complete a separate set of paperwork even though the information you are reporting is basically the same in each case. The Federal Trade Commission is taking steps to establish a uniform version of a fraud report that can be used with each vendor and creditor affected by your case.[37] Such a form would reduce your paperwork and effort by requiring all parties to accept the FTC form in lieu of their own individual report forms. In the meantime:

- Be prepared to fill out fraud affidavits with banks and creditors where fraudulent accounts have been established in your name.

- Do <u>not</u> cancel your unaffected credit cards- that is, the ones that the thieves missed. Because your credit has been tarnished or destroyed you may have problems when attempting to open new lines of credit. Keep what you can!

- Victims can request that credit bureaus place a fraud alert on their credit report. This is no guarantee against future fraud because the alerts may not be displayed prominently enough to draw the attention of creditors. Many times, creditors order credit scores as opposed to an entire credit report, and information of the fraud alert is never forwarded.

Your Liability

Your liability differs, depending on how the identity theft occurs. For example, if someone uses your ATM card to fraudulently withdraw money from your bank account, the Electronic Funds Transfer Act limits your losses to $50 if you report the theft within two business days. If you wait between 2-60 days of discovering the loss, you can be liable for up to $500 of what a criminal withdraws. If you wait 60 days after receiving a bank statement that includes an unauthorized transfer, the law doesn't require your bank to reimburse you for any losses. However, you are not responsible for any funds after you inform the bank that your ATM card is lost or stolen.[38]

If your credit card is used fraudulently, your liability is limited to $50 per card under the Fair

Credit Billing Act. The Act also establishes procedures for resolving billing errors on your credit card accounts. A victim's liability for unauthorized use of a debit card is similar to that of a credit card.

Under the Fair Credit Reporting Act, you have the right to dispute inaccurate information contained within your credit file. The credit bureaus must conduct an investigation if you inform them of incorrect information. If you disagree with the results of the investigation, you may add a brief statement to your file, which gives your version of what actually occurred.

Also, as the victim you have a right to the signed document in cases involving disputed charges. This is the single most effective way to challenge and disprove a vendor's allegations that you made charges which you did not, in fact, make. Also, thanks to recent legislation, you can now get the help of the police in analyzing the handwriting on transactions which are in dispute.[39]

You also have the right to take creditors to court if they hound you about charges that you have disputed. Once you've informed them that you are a victim identity theft and send a creditor the police report, they must cease and desist.[40]

The Guide to Identity Theft Prevention
The Importance of Documentation

Document everything! This should be obvious by now. Keep a detailed log of everything you do in your dealings with creditors, investigators, law enforcement authorities, etc. Maintain copies of letters and documents and send all correspondence by certified mail. Keep a record of phone conversations. Make sure they include:

- Name of the person you spoke with
- Time and date of the call
- Phone number
- Topic of discussion

The following is a list of key documents you should keep on file:[41]

- Police report
- Chronological and detailed journal of events
- Any applications, credit slips, credit cards, physical proof of fraud
- Credit reports
- Telephone records
- Costs
- Copies of all letters you send or receive regarding the case
- All court documents

- Victim statements
- Court notes
- Summary of case to date

Checking and savings accounts: If you have reason to believe that an identity thief has accessed your checking or savings account, close the accounts immediately and obtain new account numbers. If you have had checks stolen or bank accounts set up fraudulently, report it to the check verification companies:

- CheckRite (800) 766-2748
- ChexSystems (800) 428-9623 (regarding closed bank account only)
- Equifax Check Services (800) 437-5120
- National Processing Co. (800) 526-5380
- TeleCheck (800) 710-9898

Stop payment on any outstanding checks you are unsure of. If your ATM card has been lost, stolen, or compromised, cancel the card and get another with a new PIN. Ask for a secret password that must be used before every transaction

Other steps:

- Notify the passport office and inform them you have been the victim of identity theft.

The Guide to Identity Theft Prevention

Tell them to be on the lookout for anyone ordering a passport fraudulently using your name and identification.
- When requesting a new drivers licenses from the department of motor vehicles, be aware that you may be asked to prove you have been damaged by the theft of your license.
- Notify postal inspectors if you suspect mail fraud.
- Contact your utility companies (gas, water, electric, and telephone) as well if you suspect fraudulent activity.
- If your social security number has been used fraudulently for employment purposes, report the problem to the Social Security Administration at (800) 680-7293. You may order your Earnings and Benefits Statement by calling (800) 772-1213. Be advised, however, that the Administration deals only with employment-related fraud; it does not deal with situations where your social security number has been used in other types of situations such as purchases.[42]

Chapter 8

Identity Theft Case Files

This section will outline several actual cases.

Mail theft in Colorado. A group of Colorado apartment complexes had over 500 mailboxes broken into by mail thieves over a period of one month. The thieves used a screwdriver or some other tool to pry open the mailboxes at the apartment buildings. One resident was surprised when she discovered her $22 credit card payment had been removed from her mailbox, washed and cashed for $800 at a local bank.[43]

Airport credit card scam. Travelers passing through Vancouver International Airport lost hundreds of thousands of dollars to a credit card scam operating at the international gate. Informed that they had to pay an airport improvement fee-it was indeed a legitimate fee-the passengers turned over their credit cards. The criminals would double swipe the credit cards, once through the legitimate machine and once through an illegal device that recorded the credit card account

The Guide to Identity Theft Prevention

number. People would get their cards back not knowing what had occurred.

Once the credit card number was recorded, it was downloaded and reproduced on a fake card and used for various types of purchases. Police were alerted by a credit card company concerned with a high number of abnormal charges, which appeared after the airport improvement had been paid.[44]

ID theft at the DMV. Several employees at a state department of motor vehicles were allegedly bribed to "clean" car titles, alter the vehicle identification numbers on cars and in some cases create new identities. One employee allegedly took payments of $150 to $200. In exchange, the employee issued state identifications or drivers licenses to applicants who lacked the required documentation. The employee also falsified or altered information in the records including dates of birth, social security numbers and addresses-and created illegal titles for cars that were stolen or that had been resold after being involved in serious accidents.[45]

Big fish at the FTC. Of all the credit card numbers in the world, a thief stole one belonging to Robert Pitofsky, a top federal regulator of the credit card industry and the Chairman of the

Federal Trade Commission.[46] Pitofsky disclosed that someone stole his official government credit card in 1998 and ran up charges buying mail order items from catalogs.

Lone Star credit demon. When a Wisconsin woman and her husband went to the bank to refinance their home, they thought it would be routine, After all, they were refinancing with their existing mortgage lenders and they had good credit-or so they thought. They were shocked when the bank officer turned them down and pointed to their credit report. A woman in Texas had applied for credit 19 times using the victim's name and social security number. She made purchases totaling $60,000.[47]

Relative steals woman's identity. After her military clearance was suddenly suspended, an army employee discovered that a relative had stolen her identity and opened several fraudulent accounts. In an effort to clear herself, she paid off $30,000 in fraudulent debts. She then quit her job to get a new, better paying job, but the offer was subsequently withdrawn after the prospective employer saw her credit report. As a result, she was left jobless and unable to maintain her apartment. She was unable to gain any type of government assistance or financial assistance from

The Guide to Identity Theft Prevention

the credit bureaus involved. Ultimately, she had to leave the country because the only employment she was able to obtain was in Korea.[48]

$250,000 spending spree. One identity thief was opening bank accounts under several identities-usually with stolen drivers licenses and social security numbers. With those, he was able to deposit stolen or forged high dollar checks, withdrawing some or all of the money before the check cleared. Every month or so, he'd move on to a new alias and a new checking account. The FBI was investigating one alias and the Secret Service was investigating another; what they didn't know is that they were investigating the same person. The criminal was eventually caught, putting an end to his $250,000 spending spree.[49]

Her precautions were not enough. A 34-year old surgeon had her purse stolen from a locked desk at the hospital where she was employed. She quickly canceled her credit cards and checks. About two years later she received a phone call from a collection agency about an overdue account of $3,500 from an out-of-state jewelry store. A copy of her credit report revealed that almost $30,000 worth of jewelry, roaming cell phone charges and department store charges had been made in her name.[50]

Johnny R. May

Trafficking in new credit card accounts. One afternoon a California woman was feeding her one-year-old daughter when the telephone rang. The credit card company informed her someone had applied for a credit card in her name and it didn't match the addresses they had for her. Someone had already used the credit card, acquired over the Internet without her knowledge to make almost $500 in unauthorized purchases. Months passed, and soon she discovered more than three dozen of her former co-workers at a pharmaceuticals company had also become victims of identity theft. The group discovered that their identities were used to illegally obtain about 75 credit cards, buy at least $100,000 in merchandise, open 20 cellular telephone accounts and rent three apartments.[51]

Will the real mother please pay the bill? A Florida woman was recently charged with assuming a former neighbor's identity and insurance when she admitted herself into a hospital for the delivery of her baby. The victim, a Texas woman, contacted police after receiving a series of phone calls from a Florida hospital demanding payment for delivery of her child. The accused also had opened utilities and bank accounts in the victim's name.[52]

Does Grandma really need all those phones? Seniors are often targeted. Creditors were shocked to learn that the purported owner of five Nextel phones was an infirm, 93-year-old woman who required around-the-clock care.[53]

The enterprising data entry clerk. A data entry clerk in Tampa, Florida, who had access to sensitive personal information was accused of stealing the identities of 350 people. The woman was arrested after trying to make a fraudulent purchase with a credit card. Inside her car, police found what they described as 350 "complete identities" including victim names, addresses, social security numbers and dates of birth.[54]

Identity theft murder. In Detroit, a woman was actually murdered in a bizarre case of identity theft! The perpetrator, a woman with a troubled past, had been a co-worker of the victim. This identity thief hired her nephew and a friend to kill the victim-but changed the dead woman's identity to her own. When police found the victim's body, the perpetrator persuaded them that she was the victim's sister-i.e., her own sister! The scheme unraveled a couple days later when police brought the identity thief's relatives to the funeral home and they did not recognize the dead woman.[55]

Preying on cancer patients. A former employee at one of the country's leading cancer centers, located in Boston, was recently charged with stealing the social security numbers and other information she gathered from patients. The woman worked for about four months after being hired through a temporary agency. A mass mailing was sent to 12,000 people who were admitted for treatment while the woman was working there, suggesting that they check their credit reports.[56]

Identity theft puts golf star "in the rough." Tiger Woods had to go to trial to protect his good name. Prosecutors charged Anthony Lemar Taylor of Sacramento, California, with using the golf superstar's real name-Eldrick T. Woods-and social security number to apply for credit cards and obtain a fake drivers license. The perpetrator ran up $17,000 in credit card charges before police identified Taylor as the suspect.[57]

Moonlighting at the morgue. Ten morgue workers in Philadelphia were charged with stealing cash, credit cards, weapons, and bank and personal information from dead people. Six accomplices were also charged, because they allegedly benefited from the thefts by processing the stolen credit cards and opening new accounts in the names of the deceased. The investigation was prompted when a woman discovered that someone had used her dead father's credit cards and opened new accounts in his name.[58]

Johnny R. May

Appendices

Johnny R. May

OK TO COPY THIS APPENDIX

Appendix A: Credit Bureaus

Requesting Credit Reports and Reporting Fraud

Following are the three major credit bureaus that maintain credit history on consumers. You should contact these organizations when you wish to get a copy of your credit report or if you have questions about your credit history. There is often a fee for this service. However, if you have been denied credit, you are entitled by law to receive a free credit report from each credit bureau. Also, the law now requires that victims of identity theft receive free annual credit reports.

EQUIFAX
P. O. Box 105873
Atlanta, GA 30348
Order credit report: (800) 685-1111
Report fraud: (800) 525-6285
Web site: www.equifax.com

EXPERIAN (formerly TRW)
P. O. Box 2104
Allen, TX 75013-2104
Order credit report: (888) 397-3742
Report fraud: (800) 301-7195
Web site: www.experian.com

TRANSUNION CORPORATION
P. O. 34012
Fullerton, CA 92834
Order credit report: (800) 916-8800
Report fraud: (800) 680-7289
Web site: www.tuc.com

On the following page is a sample letter that can be used to ask these bureaus to refrain from selling your name and address to advertisers.

Johnny R. May

OK TO PHOTOCOPY THIS APPENDIX

Letter Requesting Removal from Marketing Lists

Date
To whom it may concern:
I request to have my name removed from your marketing lists. Following is the information you have asked me to include in my request.

FIRST, MIDDLE & LAST NAME*(List all name variations, including Jr., Sr., etc.)*

CURRENT MAILING ADDRESS

PREVIOUS MAILING ADDRESS*(Fill in your previous mailing address if you have moved in the last 6 months.)**Note: not required by Equifax and Experian.*

SOCIAL SECURITY NUMBER*Note: not required by Experian.*

DATE OF BIRTH*Note: not required by Equifax and Experian.*

Thank you for your prompt handling of my request.

_____**SIGNATURE**

The Guide to Identity Theft Prevention

OK TO COPY THIS APPENDIX

Appendix B: Resources

Following are some organizations, publications and websites that have information or perform services that can be helpful to victims of identity theft, as well as to those who are interested in prevention strategies.

Organizations

Federal Trade Commission
600 Pennsylvania Avenue, NW
Washington, DC 20580
www.consumer.gov/idtheft

CALPIRG
11965 Venice Blvd., Suite 408,
Los Angeles, CA 90066.
Phone: (310) 397-3404 or (916) 448-4516.
E-mail: calpirg@pirg.org
Web site: www.pirg.org/calpirg

Johnny R. May

Identity Theft Prevention and Survival
28202 Cabot Road, Suite 215,
Laguna Niguel, 92677
Contact: Mari J. Frank, Esq.,
Author, *The Identity Theft Survival Kit*
Phone 800-725-0807 or 949-364-1511
E-mail contact@identitytheft.org
Web site: www.identitytheft.org

Privacy Rights Clearinghouse
1717 Kettner Ave., Ste. 105,
San Diego, CA 2101
Phone: (619) 298-3396
Contact: Director, Beth Givens
E-mail: prc@privacyrights.org
Web site: www.privacyrights.org

Publications

Privacy Times
P.O. Box 21501
Washington, D.C. 20009
PHONE: (202) 829-3660
FAX (202) 829-3653
e-mail: evan@privacytimes.com

Privacy Journal
P.O. Box 28577
Providence, RI 02908
Phone: 401-274-7861
e-mail: privacyjournal@prodigy.net

Fraud Prevention Manual: 5 Steps to Prevent Stolen Identity Credit Fraud
by Travis Perry
The Future Crime Prevention Association
P.O.Box 4416
Victoria, Texas 77903
Website: www.futurecrime.com

Identity Theft: The Cybercrime of the Milennium
by John Q. Newman
Loompanics Unlimited
PO Box 1197
Port Townsend, WA 98368
Website: www.loompanics.com

From Victor to Victim:
A Step-by-Step Guide for Ending the Nightmare of Identity Theft
by Mari Frank
Porpoise Press
28202 Cabot Road, Suite 215
Laguna Niguel, CA 92677
Website: www.identitytheft.org

The Privacy Rights Handbook: How to Take Control of Your Personal Information
by Beth Givens
Avon Books
1350 Avenue of the Americas
New York, New York 10019
Website: www.AvonBooks.com

Identity Theft Websites

ID Theft Services

www.idfraud.com

GrandTheft.com

www.grandtheft.com

Privacy Rights Clearinghouse

www.privacyrights.org

Identity Theft Prevention & Survival

www.identitytheft.org

Federal Trade Commission Identity Theft Information

www.consumer.gov/idtheft/

U.S. Department of Justice: Identity Theft & Fraud

www.usdoj.gov/criminal/fraud/idtheft.html

Free Information on Identity Theft

www.stolen-identity.com

Information Page on Identity Theft

www.home.pon.net/dumpdude/idtheft.html

Identity Crisis

http://mason.gmu.edu/~jpage/

National Fraud Center

www.nationalfraud.com

Victims of Credit Reporting

www.vcr.org

OK TO COPY THIS APPENDIX

Appendix C: Check Verification Companies

If you have had checks stolen or bank accounts set up fraudulently, report it to these check verification companies:

- CheckRite (800) 766-2748

- ChexSystems (800) 428-9623 (regarding closed bank account only)

- Equifax Check Services (800) 437-5120

- National Processing Co. (800) 526-5380

- TeleCheck (800) 710-9898

Johnny R. May

OK TO COPY THIS APPENDIX

Appendix D: Affidavit of Fraud

WITNESSETH:

I, _____ being of sound mind and body hereby depose and say:

(1) I reside at _____ (address), _____ (city-state-zip), and that my social security number is_____. I was born on _____.

(2) I did not use, nor did I authorize anyone else to use, my name or identification to apply for credit or make charges on said credit obtained unlawfully.

(3) I hereby agree to cooperate with your fraud unit and any law enforcement agency in the prosecution of the individual who applied for credit and used that credit in my name without authorization, and in any civil action which may be brought to recover damages.

IN WITNESS WHEREOF, I hereunto set my hand this____day of _____, _____

Signed_____

STATE OF _____ COUNTY OF _____

I, _____, residing in the county and state aforesaid, do certify that _____, who is personally known, this day appeared before me personally and did acknowledge that he did sign, seal and deliver the foregoing instrument of his free will and accord, for the purpose therein named and expressed.

IN WITNESS WHEREOF, I have hereunto set my hand and official seal, this _____ day of _____, _____.
Signed _____, Notary Public
My Commission Expires _____

The Guide to Identity Theft Prevention
OK TO COPY THIS APPENDIX

Appendix E: Letter of Dispute—Template

Date:

Your Name
Your Street address
Your City, State Zip Code

Fraud Victim Assistance Division
Credit Bureau
Street address
City, State Zip Code

Dear Sir or Madam,

    I am writing to dispute the following information in my file. The items I dispute are circled on the attached copy of the report I received. The first discrepancy is **(Be as specific and detailed as you can. Tell them exactly what you are disputing and why)**. I am requesting that these items be deleted to correct the errors in my credit report. **(Start the dispute process way before you get the police report.)**
    Enclosed are copies of the credit report with discrepancies circled. **(Provide all the documentation you can get your hands on.)** Please investigate these matters and delete the disputed items as soon as possible.

Sincerely,

Your Name

Enclosures: **(List copies you have enclosed)**

Johnny R. May

OK TO COPY THIS APPENDIX

Appendix F: Creditor Dispute Letter—Template

Date:

Your Name
Street Address
City, State Zip

Creditor's Title
Street Address
City, State Zip

Dear Sir or Madam,

I am writing to clear my name and false bad credit as I am a victim of identity theft. Some one in **(indicate State)** has used my social security number and name to illegally open an account. I have never had an account with **(creditor's name)**. I am requesting that the fraudulent account be removed from my name and damages or losses be recovered from the identity thief.

Enclosed is **(tell them what enclosures you have)**. Please investigate this matter and correct the damage done by the identity thief as soon as possible.

Sincerely

Your Name

Enclosures: (List Enclosures)

OK TO COPY THIS APPENDIX

Appendix G: State Statutes Relating to Identity Theft

As of February, 2001, these were the various state statutes which related to identity theft. NOTE: Laws have changed dramatically since 1998, both at the state and the federal level, and they continue to do so. Therefore, you should confer with your state attorney general's office for the latest information about laws in your state. Most of these statutes may be reviewed online. Go to the website for your state government for further information.

Arizona	Ariz. Rev. Stat. ' 13-2708
Arkansas Ark.	Code Ann. ' 5-37-227
California	Cal. Penal Code ' 530.5
Connecticut	1999 Conn. Acts 99-99
Delaware	Del. Code Ann. tit. 11, ' 854
Florida	Fla. Stat. Ann. ' 817.568
Georgia	Ga. Code Ann. " 121-127
Idaho	Idaho Code ' 28-3126
Illinois	720 ILCS 5/16G
Indiana	Ind.Code ' 35-43-5-4 (2000)
Iowa	Iowa Code ' 715A.8)

Kansas	Kan. Stat. Ann. ' 21-4108
Kentucky	2000 Ky. Acts ' 1, ch. 514
Louisiana	La. Rev. Stat. Ann. ' 67.16
Maine	Me. Rev. Stat. Ann. tit. 17-A, ' 354-2A
Maryland	Md. Ann. Code art. 27, ' 231
Massachusetts	1998 Mass. Acts 397 (to be codified at Mass. Gen. Laws ch. 266, ' 37E)
Minnesota	Minn. Stat. Ann. ' 609.527
Mississippi	Miss. Code Ann. ' 97-19-85
Missouri	Mo. Rev. Stat. ' 570.223
Nebraska	Neb. Rev. State. ' 28-101
Nevada	Nev. Rev. State. ' 205.465
New Hampshire	N.H. Rev. Stat. Ann. ' 638:26
New Jersey	N.J. Stat. Ann. ' 2C:21-17
North Carolina	N.C. Gen. Stat. ' 14-113.20
North Dakota	N.D.C.C. ' 12.1-23-11
Ohio	Ohio Rev. Code Ann. 2913.49
Oklahoma	Okla. Stat. tit. 21, ' 1533.1
Oregon	Or. Rev. Stat. ' 165.800
Rhode Island	R.I. Gen. Laws ' 11-49.1-1
South Carolina	S.C. Code Ann. ' 16-13-500
Tennessee	Tenn. Code Ann. ' 39-14-150
Texas	Senate Bill 46 (1999) (to be codified at Tex. Penal Code ' 32.51)
Utah	Utah Code Ann. ' 76-6-1101-1104

The Guide to Identity Theft Prevention

Virginia	VA. Code Ann. ' 18.2-186.3
Washington	Wash. Rev. Code ' 9.35 (click on title 9, then chapter 35)
West Virginia	W. Va. Code ' 61-3-54
Wisconsin	Wis. Stat. ' 943.201
Wyoming	Wyo. Stat. Ann. ' 6-3-901

Johnny R. May

OK TO COPY THIS APPENDIX

Appendix H: The Fair Credit Reporting Act

Since credit reporting is so critical to the consumer seeking to protect himself from identity theft, this appendix provides the complete text for the Fair Credit Reporting Act, with a brief preface from the Federal Trade Commission. In developing this law, Congress sought to address issues involving the accuracy and fairness of credit reports.

The Fair Credit Reporting Act As a public service, the staff of the Federal Trade Commission (FTC) has prepared the following complete text of the Fair Credit Reporting Act (FCRA), 15 U.S.C. ' 1681 *et seq*. Although staff generally followed the format of the U.S. Code as published by the Government Printing Office, the format of this text does differ in minor ways from the Code (and from West's U.S. Code Annotated). For example, this version uses FCRA section numbers (" 601-625) in the headings. (The relevant U.S. Code citation is included with each section heading and each reference to the FCRA in the text.) This version of the FCRA is complete as of July 1999. It includes the amendments to the FCRA set forth in the Consumer Credit Reporting Reform Act of 1996 (Public Law 104-208, the Omnibus Consolidated Appropriations Act for Fiscal Year 1997, Title II, Subtitle D, Chapter 1), Section 311 of the Intelligence Authorization for Fiscal Year 1998 (Public Law 105-107), and the Consumer Reporting Employment Clarification Act of 1998 (Public Law 105-347). **Table of Contents** ' 601 Short title ' 602 Congressional findings and statement of purpose ' 603 Definitions; rules of construction ' 604 Permissible purposes of consumer reports ' 605 Requirements relating to information contained in consumer reports ' 606 Disclosure of

The Guide to Identity Theft Prevention

investigative consumer reports ' 607 Compliance procedures ' 608 Disclosures to governmental agencies ' 609 Disclosures to consumers ' 610 Conditions and form of disclosure to consumers ' 611 Procedure in case of disputed accuracy ' 612 Charges for certain disclosures ' 613 Public record information for employment purposes ' 614 Restrictions on investigative consumer reports ' 615 Requirements on users of consumer reports ' 616 Civil liability for willful noncompliance ' 617 Civil liability for negligent noncompliance ' 618 Jurisdiction of courts; limitation of actions ' 619 Obtaining information under false pretenses ' 620 Unauthorized disclosures by officers or employees ' 621 Administrative enforcement ' 622 Information on overdue child support obligations ' 623 Responsibilities of furnishers of information to consumer reporting agencies ' 624 Relation to State laws ' 625 Disclosures to FBI for counterintelligence purposes ' **601. Short title** This title may be cited as the Fair Credit Reporting Act. ' **602. Congressional findings and statement of purpose** [15 U.S.C. ' 1681] (a) Accuracy and fairness of credit reporting. The Congress makes the following findings: (1) The banking system is dependent upon fair and accurate credit reporting. Inaccurate credit reports directly impair the efficiency of the banking system, and unfair credit reporting methods undermine the public confidence which is essential to the continued functioning of the banking system. (2) An elaborate mechanism has been developed for investigating and evaluating the credit worthiness, credit standing, credit capacity, character, and general reputation of consumers. (3) Consumer reporting agencies have assumed a vital role in assembling and evaluating consumer credit and other information on consumers. (4) There is a need to insure that consumer reporting agencies exercise their grave responsibilities with fairness, impartiality, and a respect for the consumer's right to privacy. (b) Reasonable procedures. It is the purpose of this title to require that consumer reporting agencies adopt reasonable procedures for meeting the needs of commerce for consumer credit, personnel, insurance, and other information in a manner which is fair and equitable to the consumer, with regard to the confidentiality, accuracy, relevancy, and proper utilization of such information in accordance with the requirements of this title. ' **603. Definitions; rules of construction** [15 U.S.C. ' 1681a] (a) Definitions and rules of construction set forth in this section are applicable for the purposes of this title. (b) The term "person" means any individual, partnership, corporation, trust, estate, cooperative, association, government or governmental subdivision or agency, or other entity. (c) The term "consumer" means an individual. (d) Consumer report. (1) In general. The term "consumer report" means any written, oral, or other communication of any information by a

Johnny R. May

consumer reporting agency bearing on a consumer's credit worthiness, credit standing, credit capacity, character, general reputation, personal characteristics, or mode of living which is used or expected to be used or collected in whole or in part for the purpose of serving as a factor in establishing the consumer's eligibility for (A) credit or insurance to be used primarily for personal, family, or household purposes; (B) employment purposes; or (C) any other purpose authorized under section 604 [' 1681b]. (2) Exclusions. The term "consumer report" does not include (A) any (i) report containing information solely as to transactions or experiences between the consumer and the person making the report; (ii) communication of that information among persons related by common ownership or affiliated by corporate control; or (iii) communication of other information among persons related by common ownership or affiliated by corporate control, if it is clearly and conspicuously disclosed to the consumer that the information may be communicated among such persons and the consumer is given the opportunity, before the time that the information is initially communicated, to direct that such information not be communicated among such persons; (B) any authorization or approval of a specific extension of credit directly or indirectly by the issuer of a credit card or similar device; (C) any report in which a person who has been requested by a third party to make a specific extension of credit directly or indirectly to a consumer conveys his or her decision with respect to such request, if the third party advises the consumer of the name and address of the person to whom the request was made, and such person makes the disclosures to the consumer required under section 615 [' 1681m]; or (D) a communication described in subsection (o). (e) The term "investigative consumer report" means a consumer report or portion thereof in which information on a consumer's character, general reputation, personal characteristics, or mode of living is obtained through personal interviews with neighbors, friends, or associates of the consumer reported on or with others with whom he is acquainted or who may have knowledge concerning any such items of information. However, such information shall not include specific factual information on a consumer's credit record obtained directly from a creditor of the consumer or from a consumer reporting agency when such information was obtained directly from a creditor of the consumer or from the consumer. (f) The term "consumer reporting agency" means any person which, for monetary fees, dues, or on a cooperative nonprofit basis, regularly engages in whole or in part in the practice of assembling or evaluating consumer credit information or other information on consumers for the purpose of furnishing consumer reports to third parties, and which uses any means or facility of

The Guide to Identity Theft Prevention

interstate commerce for the purpose of preparing or furnishing consumer reports. (g) The term "file," when used in connection with information on any consumer, means all of the information on that consumer recorded and retained by a consumer reporting agency regardless of how the information is stored. (h) The term "employment purposes" when used in connection with a consumer report means a report used for the purpose of evaluating a consumer for employment, promotion, reassignment or retention as an employee. (i) The term "medical information" means information or records obtained, with the consent of the individual to whom it relates, from licensed physicians or medical practitioners, hospitals, clinics, or other medical or medically related facilities. (j) Definitions relating to child support obligations. (1) Overdue support. The term "overdue support" has the meaning given to such term in section 666(e) of title 42 [Social Security Act, 42 U.S.C. ' 666(e)]. (2) State or local child support enforcement agency. The term "State or local child support enforcement agency" means a State or local agency which administers a State or local program for establishing and enforcing child support obligations. (k) Adverse action. (1) Actions included. The term "adverse action" (A) has the same meaning as in section 701(d)(6) of the Equal Credit Opportunity Act; and (B) means (i) a denial or cancellation of, an increase in any charge for, or a reduction or other adverse or unfavorable change in the terms of coverage or amount of, any insurance, existing or applied for, in connection with the underwriting of insurance; (ii) a denial of employment or any other decision for employment purposes that adversely affects any current or prospective employee; (iii) a denial or cancellation of, an increase in any charge for, or any other adverse or unfavorable change in the terms of, any license or benefit described in section 604(a)(3)(D) [' 1681b]; and (iv) an action taken or determination that is (I) made in connection with an application that was made by, or a transaction that was initiated by, any consumer, or in connection with a review of an account under section 604(a)(3)(F)(ii)[' 1681b]; and (II) adverse to the interests of the consumer. (2) Applicable findings, decisions, commentary, and orders. For purposes of any determination of whether an action is an adverse action under paragraph (1)(A), all appropriate final findings, decisions, commentary, and orders issued under section 701(d)(6) of the Equal Credit Opportunity Act by the Board of Governors of the Federal Reserve System or any court shall apply. (l) Firm offer of credit or insurance. The term "firm offer of credit or insurance" means any offer of credit or insurance to a consumer that will be honored if the consumer is determined, based on information in a consumer report on the consumer, to meet the specific criteria used to select the consumer

Johnny R. May

for the offer, except that the offer may be further conditioned on one or more of the following: (1) The consumer being determined, based on information in the consumer's application for the credit or insurance, to meet specific criteria bearing on credit worthiness or insurability, as applicable, that are established (A) before selection of the consumer for the offer; and (B) for the purpose of determining whether to extend credit or insurance pursuant to the offer. (2) Verification (A) that the consumer continues to meet the specific criteria used to select the consumer for the offer, by using information in a consumer report on the consumer, information in the consumer's application for the credit or insurance, or other information bearing on the credit worthiness or insurability of the consumer; or (B) of the information in the consumer's application for the credit or insurance, to determine that the consumer meets the specific criteria bearing on credit worthiness or insurability. (3) The consumer furnishing any collateral that is a requirement for the extension of the credit or insurance that was (A) established before selection of the consumer for the offer of credit or insurance; and (B) disclosed to the consumer in the offer of credit or insurance. (m) Credit or insurance transaction that is not initiated by the consumer. The term "credit or insurance transaction that is not initiated by the consumer" does not include the use of a consumer report by a person with which the consumer has an account or insurance policy, for purposes of (1) reviewing the account or insurance policy; or (2) collecting the account. (n) State. The term "State" means any State, the Commonwealth of Puerto Rico, the District of Columbia, and any territory or possession of the United States. (o) Excluded communications. A communication is described in this subsection if it is a communication (1) that, but for subsection (d)(2)(D), would be an investigative consumer report; (2) that is made to a prospective employer for the purpose of (A) procuring an employee for the employer; or (B) procuring an opportunity for a natural person to work for the employer; (3) that is made by a person who regularly performs such procurement; (4) that is not used by any person for any purpose other than a purpose described in subparagraph (A) or (B) of paragraph (2); and (5) with respect to which (A) the consumer who is the subject of the communication (i) consents orally or in writing to the nature and scope of the communication, before the collection of any information for the purpose of making the communication; (ii) consents orally or in writing to the making of the communication to a prospective employer, before the making of the communication; and (iii) in the case of consent under clause (i) or (ii) given orally, is provided written confirmation of that consent by the person making the communication, not later than 3 business days after the receipt of the consent by that

The Guide to Identity Theft Prevention

person; (B) the person who makes the communication does not, for the purpose of making the communication, make any inquiry that if made by a prospective employer of the consumer who is the subject of the communication would violate any applicable Federal or State equal employment opportunity law or regulation; and (C) the person who makes the communication (i) discloses in writing to the consumer who is the subject of the communication, not later than 5 business days after receiving any request from the consumer for such disclosure, the nature and substance of all information in the consumer's file at the time of the request, except that the sources of any information that is acquired solely for use in making the communication and is actually used for no other purpose, need not be disclosed other than under appropriate discovery procedures in any court of competent jurisdiction in which an action is brought; and (ii) notifies the consumer who is the subject of the communication, in writing, of the consumer's right to request the information described in clause (i). (p) Consumer reporting agency that compiles and maintains files on consumers on a nationwide basis. The term "consumer reporting agency that compiles and maintains files on consumers on a nationwide basis" means a consumer reporting agency that regularly engages in the practice of assembling or evaluating, and maintaining, for the purpose of furnishing consumer reports to third parties bearing on a consumer's credit worthiness, credit standing, or credit capacity, each of the following regarding consumers residing nationwide: (1) Public record information. (2) Credit account information from persons who furnish that information regularly and in the ordinary course of business. ' **604. Permissible purposes of consumer reports** [15 U.S.C. ' 1681b] (a) In general. Subject to subsection (c), any consumer reporting agency may furnish a consumer report under the following circumstances and no other: (1) In response to the order of a court having jurisdiction to issue such an order, or a subpoena issued in connection with proceedings before a Federal grand jury. (2) In accordance with the written instructions of the consumer to whom it relates. (3) To a person which it has reason to believe (A) intends to use the information in connection with a credit transaction involving the consumer on whom the information is to be furnished and involving the extension of credit to, or review or collection of an account of, the consumer; or (B) intends to use the information for employment purposes; or (C) intends to use the information in connection with the underwriting of insurance involving the consumer; or (D) intends to use the information in connection with a determination of the consumer's eligibility for a license or other benefit granted by a governmental instrumentality required by law to consider an applicant's financial responsibility or status; or (E) intends to use the information, as a potential investor or servicer, or current insurer, in connection with a valuation of, or an assessment of the credit or prepayment risks associated with, an existing credit obligation; or (F) otherwise has a legitimate business need for the information (i) in connection with a business transaction that is initiated by the consumer; or (ii) to review an account to determine whether the consumer continues to meet the terms of the account. (4) In response to a request by the head of a State or local child support enforcement agency (or a State or local government official authorized by the head of such an agency), if the person making the request certifies to the consumer reporting agency that (A) the consumer report is needed for the purpose of establishing an individual's capacity to make child support payments or determining the appropriate level of such payments; (B) the paternity of the consumer for the child to which the obligation relates has been established or acknowledged by the consumer in accordance with State laws under which the obligation arises (if required by those laws); (C) the person has provided at least 10 days' prior notice to the consumer whose report is requested, by certified or registered mail to the last known address of the consumer, that the report will be requested; and (D) the consumer report will be kept confidential, will be used solely for a purpose described in subparagraph (A), and will not be used in connection with any other civil, administrative, or criminal proceeding, or for any other purpose. (5) To an agency administering a State plan under Section 454 of the Social Security Act (42 U.S.C. ' 654) for use to set an initial or modified child support award. (b) Conditions for furnishing and using consumer reports for employment purposes. (1) Certification from user. A consumer reporting agency may furnish a consumer report for employment purposes only if (A) the person who obtains such report from the agency certifies to the agency that (i) the person has complied with paragraph (2) with respect to the consumer report, and the person will comply with paragraph (3) with respect to the consumer report if paragraph (3) becomes applicable; and (ii) information from the consumer report will not be used in violation of any applicable Federal or State equal employment opportunity law or regulation; and (B) the consumer reporting agency provides with the report, or has previously provided, a summary of the consumer's rights under this title, as prescribed by the Federal Trade Commission under section 609(c)(3) [' 1681g]. (2) Disclosure to consumer. (A) In general. Except as provided in subparagraph (B), a person may not procure a consumer report, or cause a consumer report to be procured, for employment purposes with respect to any consumer, unless— (i) a clear and conspicuous disclosure has been made in writing to the consumer at

The Guide to Identity Theft Prevention

any time before the report is procured or caused to be procured, in a document that consists solely of the disclosure, that a consumer report may be obtained for employment purposes; and (ii) the consumer has authorized in writing (which authorization may be made on the document referred to in clause (i)) the procurement of the report by that person. (B) Application by mail, telephone, computer, or other similar means. If a consumer described in subparagraph (C) applies for employment by mail, telephone, computer, or other similar means, at any time before a consumer report is procured or caused to be procured in connection with that application— (i) the person who procures the consumer report on the consumer for employment purposes shall provide to the consumer, by oral, written, or electronic means, notice that a consumer report may be obtained for employment purposes, and a summary of the consumer's rights under section 615(a)(3); and (ii) the consumer shall have consented, orally, in writing, or electronically to the procurement of the report by that person. (C) Scope. Subparagraph (B) shall apply to a person procuring a consumer report on a consumer in connection with the consumer's application for employment only if— (i) the consumer is applying for a position over which the Secretary of Transportation has the power to establish qualifications and maximum hours of service pursuant to the provisions of section 31502 of title 49, or a position subject to safety regulation by a State transportation agency; and (ii) as of the time at which the person procures the report or causes the report to be procured the only interaction between the consumer and the person in connection with that employment application has been by mail, telephone, computer, or other similar means. (3) Conditions on use for adverse actions. (A) In general. Except as provided in subparagraph (B), in using a consumer report for employment purposes, before taking any adverse action based in whole or in part on the report, the person intending to take such adverse action shall provide to the consumer to whom the report relates— (i) a copy of the report; and (ii) a description in writing of the rights of the consumer under this title, as prescribed by the Federal Trade Commission under section 609(c)(3). (B) Application by mail, telephone, computer, or other similar means. (i) If a consumer described in subparagraph (C) applies for employment by mail, telephone, computer, or other similar means, and if a person who has procured a consumer report on the consumer for employment purposes takes adverse action on the employment application based in whole or in part on the report, then the person must provide to the consumer to whom the report relates, in lieu of the notices required under subparagraph (A) of this section and under section 615(a), within 3 business days of taking such action, an oral, written or electronic notification— (I) that adverse action has been taken based in whole or in part on a consumer report received from a consumer reporting agency; (II) of the name, address and telephone number of the consumer reporting agency that furnished the consumer report (including a toll-free telephone number established by the agency if the agency compiles and maintains files on consumers on a nationwide basis); (III) that the consumer reporting agency did not make the decision to take the adverse action and is unable to provide to the consumer the specific reasons why the adverse action was taken; and (IV) that the consumer may, upon providing proper identification, request a free copy of a report and may dispute with the consumer reporting agency the accuracy or completeness of any information in a report. (ii) If, under clause (B)(i)(IV), the consumer requests a copy of a consumer report from the person who procured the report, then, within 3 business days of receiving the consumer's request, together with proper identification, the person must send or provide to the consumer a copy of a report and a copy of the consumer's rights as prescribed by the Federal Trade Commission under section 609(c)(3). (C) Scope. Subparagraph (B) shall apply to a person procuring a consumer report on a consumer in connection with the consumer's application for employment only if— (i) the consumer is applying for a position over which the Secretary of Transportation has the power to establish qualifications and maximum hours of service pursuant to the provisions of section 31502 of title 49, or a position subject to safety regulation by a State transportation agency; and (ii) as of the time at which the person procures the report or causes the report to be procured the only interaction between the consumer and the person in connection with that employment application has been by mail, telephone, computer, or other similar means. (4) Exception for national security investigations. (A) In general. In the case of an agency or department of the United States Government which seeks to obtain and use a consumer report for employment purposes, paragraph (3) shall not apply to any adverse action by such agency or department which is based in part on such consumer report, if the head of such agency or department makes a written finding that— (i) the consumer report is relevant to a national security investigation of such agency or department; (ii) the investigation is within the jurisdiction of such agency or department; (iii) there is reason to believe that compliance with paragraph (3) will— (I) endanger the life or physical safety of any person; (II) result in flight from prosecution; (III) result in the destruction of, or tampering with, evidence relevant to the investigation; (IV) result in the intimidation of a potential witness relevant to the investigation; (V) result in the compromise of classified

The Guide to Identity Theft Prevention

information; or (VI) otherwise seriously jeopardize or unduly delay the investigation or another official proceeding. (B) Notification of consumer upon conclusion of investigation. Upon the conclusion of a national security investigation described in subparagraph (A), or upon the determination that the exception under subparagraph (A) is no longer required for the reasons set forth in such subparagraph, the official exercising the authority in such subparagraph shall provide to the consumer who is the subject of the consumer report with regard to which such finding was made— (i) a copy of such consumer report with any classified information redacted as necessary; (ii) notice of any adverse action which is based, in part, on the consumer report; and (iii) the identification with reasonable specificity of the nature of the investigation for which the consumer report was sought. (C) Delegation by head of agency or department. For purposes of subparagraphs (A) and (B), the head of any agency or department of the United States Government may delegate his or her authorities under this paragraph to an official of such agency or department who has personnel security responsibilities and is a member of the Senior Executive Service or equivalent civilian or military rank. (D) Report to the congress. Not later than January 31 of each year, the head of each agency and department of the United States Government that exercised authority under this paragraph during the preceding year shall submit a report to the Congress on the number of times the department or agency exercised such authority during the year. (E) Definitions. For purposes of this paragraph, the following definitions shall apply: (i) Classified information. The term `classified information' means information that is protected from unauthorized disclosure under Executive Order No. 12958 or successor orders. (ii) National security investigation. The term 'national security investigation' means any official inquiry by an agency or department of the United States Government to determine the eligibility of a consumer to receive access or continued access to classified information or to determine whether classified information has been lost or compromised. (c) Furnishing reports in connection with credit or insurance transactions that are not initiated by the consumer. (1) In general. A consumer reporting agency may furnish a consumer report relating to any consumer pursuant to subparagraph (A) or (C) of subsection (a)(3) in connection with any credit or insurance transaction that is not initiated by the consumer only if (A) the consumer authorizes the agency to provide such report to such person; or (B) (i) the transaction consists of a firm offer of credit or insurance; (ii) the consumer reporting agency has complied with subsection (e); and (iii) there is not in effect an election by the consumer, made in accordance with subsection (e), to have the consumer's name and

Johnny R. May

address excluded from lists of names provided by the agency pursuant to this paragraph. (2) Limits on information received under paragraph (1)(B). A person may receive pursuant to paragraph (1)(B) only (A) the name and address of a consumer; (B) an identifier that is not unique to the consumer and that is used by the person solely for the purpose of verifying the identity of the consumer; and (C) other information pertaining to a consumer that does not identify the relationship or experience of the consumer with respect to a particular creditor or other entity. (3) Information regarding inquiries. Except as provided in section 609(a)(5) [' 1681g], a consumer reporting agency shall not furnish to any person a record of inquiries in connection with a credit or insurance transaction that is not initiated by a consumer. (d) Reserved. (e) Election of consumer to be excluded from lists. (1) In general. A consumer may elect to have the consumer's name and address excluded from any list provided by a consumer reporting agency under subsection (c)(1)(B) in connection with a credit or insurance transaction that is not initiated by the consumer, by notifying the agency in accordance with paragraph (2) that the consumer does not consent to any use of a consumer report relating to the consumer in connection with any credit or insurance transaction that is not initiated by the consumer. (2) Manner of notification. A consumer shall notify a consumer reporting agency under paragraph (1) (A) through the notification system maintained by the agency under paragraph (5); or (B) by submitting to the agency a signed notice of election form issued by the agency for purposes of this subparagraph. (3) Response of agency after notification through system. Upon receipt of notification of the election of a consumer under paragraph (1) through the notification system maintained by the agency under paragraph (5), a consumer reporting agency shall (A) inform the consumer that the election is effective only for the 2-year period following the election if the consumer does not submit to the agency a signed notice of election form issued by the agency for purposes of paragraph (2)(B); and (B) provide to the consumer a notice of election form, if requested by the consumer, not later than 5 business days after receipt of the notification of the election through the system established under paragraph (5), in the case of a request made at the time the consumer provides notification through the system. (4) Effectiveness of election. An election of a consumer under paragraph (1) (A) shall be effective with respect to a consumer reporting agency beginning 5 business days after the date on which the consumer notifies the agency in accordance with paragraph (2); (B) shall be effective with respect to a consumer reporting agency (i) subject to subparagraph (C), during the 2-year period beginning 5 business days after the date on which the consumer

The Guide to Identity Theft Prevention

notifies the agency of the election, in the case of an election for which a consumer notifies the agency only in accordance with paragraph (2)(A); or (ii) until the consumer notifies the agency under subparagraph (C), in the case of an election for which a consumer notifies the agency in accordance with paragraph (2)(B); (C) shall not be effective after the date on which the consumer notifies the agency, through the notification system established by the agency under paragraph (5), that the election is no longer effective; and (D) shall be effective with respect to each affiliate of the agency. (5) Notification system. (A) In general. Each consumer reporting agency that, under subsection (c)(1)(B), furnishes a consumer report in connection with a credit or insurance transaction that is not initiated by a consumer, shall (i) establish and maintain a notification system, including a toll-free telephone number, which permits any consumer whose consumer report is maintained by the agency to notify the agency, with appropriate identification, of the consumer's election to have the consumer's name and address excluded from any such list of names and addresses provided by the agency for such a transaction; and (ii) publish by not later than 365 days after the date of enactment of the Consumer Credit Reporting Reform Act of 1996, and not less than annually thereafter, in a publication of general circulation in the area served by the agency (I) a notification that information in consumer files maintained by the agency may be used in connection with such transactions; and (II) the address and toll-free telephone number for consumers to use to notify the agency of the consumer's election under clause (I). (B) Establishment and maintenance as compliance. Establishment and maintenance of a notification system (including a toll-free telephone number) and publication by a consumer reporting agency on the agency's own behalf and on behalf of any of its affiliates in accordance with this paragraph is deemed to be compliance with this paragraph by each of those affiliates. (6) Notification system by agencies that operate nationwide. Each consumer reporting agency that compiles and maintains files on consumers on a nationwide basis shall establish and maintain a notification system for purposes of paragraph (5) jointly with other such consumer reporting agencies. (f) Certain use or obtaining of information prohibited. A person shall not use or obtain a consumer report for any purpose unless (1) the consumer report is obtained for a purpose for which the consumer report is authorized to be furnished under this section; and (2) the purpose is certified in accordance with section 607 [' 1681e] by a prospective user of the report through a general or specific certification. (g) Furnishing reports containing medical information. A consumer reporting agency shall not furnish for employment purposes, or in connection with a credit or insurance transaction, a consumer report that contains medical information about a consumer, unless the consumer consents to the furnishing of the report. ' **605. Requirements relating to information contained in consumer reports** [15 U.S.C. ' 1681c] (a) Information excluded from consumer reports. Except as authorized under subsection (b) of this section, no consumer reporting agency may make any consumer report containing any of the following items of information: (1) Cases under title 11 [United States Code] or under the Bankruptcy Act that, from the date of entry of the order for relief or the date of adjudication, as the case may be, antedate the report by more than 10 years. (2) Civil suits, civil judgments, and records of arrest that from date of entry, antedate the report by more than seven years or until the governing statute of limitations has expired, whichever is the longer period. (3) Paid tax liens which, from date of payment, antedate the report by more than seven years. (4) Accounts placed for collection or charged to profit and loss which antedate the report by more than seven years.(1) (5) Any other adverse item of information, other than records of convictions of crimes which antedates the report by more than seven years.1 (b) Exempted cases. The provisions of subsection (a) of this section are not applicable in the case of any consumer credit report to be used in connection with (1) a credit transaction involving, or which may reasonably be expected to involve, a principal amount of $150,000 or more; (2) the underwriting of life insurance involving, or which may reasonably be expected to involve, a face amount of $150,000 or more; or (3) the employment of any individual at an annual salary which equals, or which may reasonably be expected to equal $75,000, or more. (c) Running of reporting period. (1) In general. The 7-year period referred to in paragraphs (4) and (6) ** of subsection (a) shall begin, with respect to any delinquent account that is placed for collection (internally or by referral to a third party, whichever is earlier), charged to profit and loss, or subjected to any similar action, upon the expiration of the 180-day period beginning on the date of the commencement of the delinquency which immediately preceded the collection activity, charge to profit and loss, or similar action. (2) Effective date. Paragraph (1) shall apply only to items of information added to the file of a consumer on or after the date that is 455 days after the date of enactment of the Consumer Credit Reporting Reform Act of 1996. (d) Information required to be disclosed. Any consumer reporting agency that furnishes a consumer report that contains information regarding any case involving the consumer that arises under title 11, United States Code, shall include in the report an identification of the chapter of such title 11 under which such case arises if provided by the source of the information. If any case arising

The Guide to Identity Theft Prevention

or filed under title 11, United States Code, is withdrawn by the consumer before a final judgment, the consumer reporting agency shall include in the report that such case or filing was withdrawn upon receipt of documentation certifying such withdrawal. (e) Indication of closure of account by consumer. If a consumer reporting agency is notified pursuant to section 623(a)(4) [' 1681s-2] that a credit account of a consumer was voluntarily closed by the consumer, the agency shall indicate that fact in any consumer report that includes information related to the account. (f) Indication of dispute by consumer. If a consumer reporting agency is notified pursuant to section 623(a)(3) [' 1681s-2] that information regarding a consumer who was furnished to the agency is disputed by the consumer, the agency shall indicate that fact in each consumer report that includes the disputed information. **' 606. Disclosure of investigative consumer reports** [15 U.S.C. ' 1681d] (a) Disclosure of fact of preparation. A person may not procure or cause to be prepared an investigative consumer report on any consumer unless (1) it is clearly and accurately disclosed to the consumer that an investigative consumer report including information as to his character, general reputation, personal characteristics and mode of living, whichever are applicable, may be made, and such disclosure (A) is made in a writing mailed, or otherwise delivered, to the consumer, not later than three days after the date on which the report was first requested, and (B) includes a statement informing the consumer of his right to request the additional disclosures provided for under subsection (b) of this section and the written summary of the rights of the consumer prepared pursuant to section 609(c) [' 1681g]; and (2) the person certifies or has certified to the consumer reporting agency that (A) the person has made the disclosures to the consumer required by paragraph (1); and (B) the person will comply with subsection (b). (b) Disclosure on request of nature and scope of investigation. Any person who procures or causes to be prepared an investigative consumer report on any consumer shall, upon written request made by the consumer within a reasonable period of time after the receipt by him of the disclosure required by subsection (a)(1) of this section, make a complete and accurate disclosure of the nature and scope of the investigation requested. This disclosure shall be made in a writing mailed, or otherwise delivered, to the consumer not later than five days after the date on which the request for such disclosure was received from the consumer or such report was first requested, whichever is the later. (c) Limitation on liability upon showing of reasonable procedures for compliance with provisions. No person may be held liable for any violation of subsection (a) or (b) of this section if he shows by a preponderance of the evidence that at the time of the

violation he maintained reasonable procedures to assure compliance with subsection (a) or (b) of this section. (d) Prohibitions. (1) Certification. A consumer reporting agency shall not prepare or furnish investigative consumer report unless the agency has received a certification under subsection (a)(2) from the person who requested the report. (2) Inquiries. A consumer reporting agency shall not make an inquiry for the purpose of preparing an investigative consumer report on a consumer for employment purposes if the making of the inquiry by an employer or prospective employer of the consumer would violate any applicable Federal or State equal employment opportunity law or regulation. (3) Certain public record information. Except as otherwise provided in section 613 [' 1681k], a consumer reporting agency shall not furnish an investigative consumer report that includes information that is a matter of public record and that relates to an arrest, indictment, conviction, civil judicial action, tax lien, or outstanding judgment, unless the agency has verified the accuracy of the information during the 30-day period ending on the date on which the report is furnished. (4) Certain adverse information. A consumer reporting agency shall not prepare or furnish an investigative consumer report on a consumer that contains information that is adverse to the interest of the consumer and that is obtained through a personal interview with a neighbor, friend, or associate of the consumer or with another person with whom the consumer is acquainted or who has knowledge of such item of information, unless (A) the agency has followed reasonable procedures to obtain confirmation of the information, from an additional source that has independent and direct knowledge of the information; or (B) the person interviewed is the best possible source of the information. '
607. Compliance procedures [15 U.S.C. ' 1681e] (a) Identity and purposes of credit users. Every consumer reporting agency shall maintain reasonable procedures designed to avoid violations of section 605 [' 1681c] and to limit the furnishing of consumer reports to the purposes listed under section 604 [' 1681b] of this title. These procedures shall require that prospective users of the information identify themselves, certify the purposes for which the information is sought, and certify that the information will be used for no other purpose. Every consumer reporting agency shall make a reasonable effort to verify the identity of a new prospective user and the uses certified by such prospective user prior to furnishing such user a consumer report. No consumer reporting agency may furnish a consumer report to any person if it has reasonable grounds for believing that the consumer report will not be used for a purpose listed in section 604 [' 1681b] of this title. (b) Accuracy of report. Whenever a consumer reporting agency prepares a consumer report it shall follow

The Guide to Identity Theft Prevention

reasonable procedures to assure maximum possible accuracy of the information concerning the individual about whom the report relates. (c) Disclosure of consumer reports by users allowed. A consumer reporting agency may not prohibit a user of a consumer report furnished by the agency on a consumer from disclosing the contents of the report to the consumer, if adverse action against the consumer has been taken by the user based in whole or in part on the report. (d) Notice to users and furnishers of information. (1) Notice requirement. A consumer reporting agency shall provide to any person (A) who regularly and in the ordinary course of business furnishes information to the agency with respect to any consumer; or (B) to whom a consumer report is provided by the agency; a notice of such person's responsibilities under this title. (2) Content of notice. The Federal Trade Commission shall prescribe the content of notices under paragraph (1), and a consumer reporting agency shall be in compliance with this subsection if it provides a notice under paragraph (1) that is substantially similar to the Federal Trade Commission prescription under this paragraph. (e) Procurement of consumer report for resale. (1) Disclosure. A person may not procure a consumer report for purposes of reselling the report (or any information in the report) unless the person discloses to the consumer reporting agency that originally furnishes the report (A) the identity of the end-user of the report (or information); and (B) each permissible purpose under section 604 [' 1681b] for which the report is furnished to the end-user of the report (or information). (2) Responsibilities of procurers for resale. A person who procures a consumer report for purposes of reselling the report (or any information in the report) shall (A) establish and comply with reasonable procedures designed to ensure that the report (or information) is resold by the person only for a purpose for which the report may be furnished under section 604 [' 1681b], including by requiring that each person to which the report (or information) is resold and that resells or provides the report (or information) to any other person (i) identifies each end user of the resold report (or information); (ii) certifies each purpose for which the report (or information) will be used; and (iii) certifies that the report (or information) will be used for no other purpose; and (B) before reselling the report, make reasonable efforts to verify the identifications and certifications made under subparagraph (A). (3) Resale of consumer report to a federal agency or department. Notwithstanding paragraph (1) or (2), a person who procures a consumer report for purposes of reselling the report (or any information in the report) shall not disclose the identity of the end-user of the report under paragraph (1) or (2) if — (A) the end user is an agency or department of the United States Government which procures

the report from the person for purposes of determining the eligibility of the consumer concerned to receive access or continued access to classified information (as defined in section 604(b)(4)(E)(i)); and (B) the agency or department certifies in writing to the person reselling the report that nondisclosure is necessary to protect classified information or the safety of persons employed by or contracting with, or undergoing investigation for work or contracting with the agency or department. '
608. Disclosures to governmental agencies [15 U.S.C. ' 1681f] Notwithstanding the provisions of section 604 [' 1681b] of this title, a consumer reporting agency may furnish identifying information respecting any consumer, limited to his name, address, former addresses, places of employment, or former places of employment, to a governmental agency. ' **609. Disclosures to consumers** [15 U.S.C. ' 1681g] (a) Information on file; sources; report recipients. Every consumer reporting agency shall, upon request, and subject to 610(a)(1) [' 1681h], clearly and accurately disclose to the consumer: (1) All information in the consumer's file at the time of the request, except that nothing in this paragraph shall be construed to require a consumer reporting agency to disclose to a consumer any information concerning credit scores or any other risk scores or predictors relating to the consumer. (2) The sources of the information; except that the sources of information acquired solely for use in preparing an investigative consumer report and actually used for no other purpose need not be disclosed: Provided, That in the event an action is brought under this title, such sources shall be available to the plaintiff under appropriate discovery procedures in the court in which the action is brought. (3) (A) Identification of each person (including each end-user identified under section 607(e)(1) [' 1681e]) that procured a consumer report (i) for employment purposes, during the 2-year period preceding the date on which the request is made; or (ii) for any other purpose, during the 1-year period preceding the date on which the request is made. (B) An identification of a person under subparagraph (A) shall include (i) the name of the person or, if applicable, the trade name (written in full) under which such person conducts business; and (ii) upon request of the consumer, the address and telephone number of the person. (C) Subparagraph (A) does not apply if— (i) the end user is an agency or department of the United States Government that procures the report from the person for purposes of determining the eligibility of the consumer to whom the report relates to receive access or continued access to classified information (as defined in section 604(b)(4)(E)(i)); and (ii) the head of the agency or department makes a written finding as prescribed under section 604(b)(4)(A). (4) The dates, original payees, and amounts of any checks upon which is based any adverse

The Guide to Identity Theft Prevention

characterization of the consumer, included in the file at the time of the disclosure. (5) A record of all inquiries received by the agency during the 1-year period preceding the request that identified the consumer in connection with a credit or insurance transaction that was not initiated by the consumer. (b) Exempt information. The requirements of subsection (a) of this section respecting the disclosure of sources of information and the recipients of consumer reports do not apply to information received or consumer reports furnished prior to the effective date of this title except to the extent that the matter involved is contained in the files of the consumer reporting agency on that date. (c) Summary of rights required to be included with disclosure. (1) Summary of rights. A consumer reporting agency shall provide to a consumer, with each written disclosure by the agency to the consumer under this section (A) a written summary of all of the rights that the consumer has under this title; and (B) in the case of a consumer reporting agency that compiles and maintains files on consumers on a nationwide basis, a toll-free telephone number established by the agency, at which personnel are accessible to consumers during normal business hours. (2) Specific items required to be included. The summary of rights required under paragraph (1) shall include (A) a brief description of this title and all rights of consumers under this title; (B) an explanation of how the consumer may exercise the rights of the consumer under this title; (C) a list of all Federal agencies responsible for enforcing any provision of this title and the address and any appropriate phone number of each such agency, in a form that will assist the consumer in selecting the appropriate agency; (D) a statement that the consumer may have additional rights under State law and that the consumer may wish to contact a State or local consumer protection agency or a State attorney general to learn of those rights; and (E) a statement that a consumer reporting agency is not required to remove accurate derogatory information from a consumer's file, unless the information is outdated under section 605 [' 1681c] or cannot be verified. (3) Form of summary of rights. For purposes of this subsection and any disclosure by a consumer reporting agency required under this title with respect to consumers' rights, the Federal Trade Commission (after consultation with each Federal agency referred to in section 621(b) [' 1681s]) shall prescribe the form and content of any such disclosure of the rights of consumers required under this title. A consumer reporting agency shall be in compliance with this subsection if it provides disclosures under paragraph (1) that are substantially similar to the Federal Trade Commission prescription under this paragraph. (4) Effectiveness. No disclosures shall be required under this subsection until the date on which the Federal Trade Commission prescribes the form and content of such disclosures under paragraph (3). ' **610. Conditions and form of disclosure to consumers** [15 U.S.C. ' 1681h] (a) In general. (1) Proper identification. A consumer reporting agency shall require, as a condition of making the disclosures required under section 609 [' 1681g], that the consumer furnish proper identification. (2) Disclosure in writing. Except as provided in subsection (b), the disclosures required to be made under section 609 [' 1681g] shall be provided under that section in writing. (b) Other forms of disclosure. (1) In general. If authorized by a consumer, a consumer reporting agency may make the disclosures required under 609 [' 1681g] (A) other than in writing; and (B) in such form as may be (i) specified by the consumer in accordance with paragraph (2); and (ii) available from the agency. (2) Form. A consumer may specify pursuant to paragraph (1) that disclosures under section 609 [' 1681g] shall be made (A) in person, upon the appearance of the consumer at the place of business of the consumer reporting agency where disclosures are regularly provided, during normal business hours, and on reasonable notice; (B) by telephone, if the consumer has made a written request for disclosure by telephone; (C) by electronic means, if available from the agency; or (D) by any other reasonable means that is available from the agency. (c) Trained personnel. Any consumer reporting agency shall provide trained personnel to explain to the consumer any information furnished to him pursuant to section 609 [' 1681g] of this title. (d) Persons accompanying consumer. The consumer shall be permitted to be accompanied by one other person of his choosing, who shall furnish reasonable identification. A consumer reporting agency may require the consumer to furnish a written statement granting permission to the consumer reporting agency to discuss the consumer's file in such person's presence. (e) Limitation of liability. Except as provided in sections 616 and 617 [" 1681n and 1681o] of this title, no consumer may bring any action or proceeding in the nature of defamation, invasion of privacy, or negligence with respect to the reporting of information against any consumer reporting agency, any user of information, or any person who furnishes information to a consumer reporting agency, based on information disclosed pursuant to section 609, 610, or 615 [" 1681g, 1681h, or 1681m] of this title or based on information disclosed by a user of a consumer report to or for a consumer against whom the user has taken adverse action, based in whole or in part on the report, except as to false information furnished with malice or willful intent to injure such consumer. ' **611. Procedure in case of disputed accuracy** [15 U.S.C. ' 1681i] (a) Reinvestigations of disputed information. (1) Reinvestigation required. (A) In general. If the completeness or

The Guide to Identity Theft Prevention

accuracy of any item of information contained in a consumer's file at a consumer reporting agency is disputed by the consumer and the consumer notifies the agency directly of such dispute, the agency shall reinvestigate free of charge and record the current status of the disputed information, or delete the item from the file in accordance with paragraph (5), before the end of the 30-day period beginning on the date on which the agency receives the notice of the dispute from the consumer. (B) Extension of period to reinvestigate. Except as provided in subparagraph (C), the 30-day period described in subparagraph (A) may be extended for not more than 15 additional days if the consumer reporting agency receives information from the consumer during that 30-day period that is relevant to the reinvestigation. (C) Limitations on extension of period to reinvestigate. Subparagraph (B) shall not apply to any reinvestigation in which, during the 30-day period described in subparagraph (A), the information that is the subject of the reinvestigation is found to be inaccurate or incomplete or the consumer reporting agency determines that the information cannot be verified. (2) Prompt notice of dispute to furnisher of information. (A) In general. Before the expiration of the 5-business-day period beginning on the date on which a consumer reporting agency receives notice of a dispute from any consumer in accordance with paragraph (1), the agency shall provide notification of the dispute to any person who provided any item of information in dispute, at the address and in the manner established with the person. The notice shall include all relevant information regarding the dispute that the agency has received from the consumer. (B) Provision of other information from consumer. The consumer reporting agency shall promptly provide to the person who provided the information in dispute all relevant information regarding the dispute that is received by the agency from the consumer after the period referred to in subparagraph (A) and before the end of the period referred to in paragraph (1)(A). (3) Determination that dispute is frivolous or irrelevant. (A) In general. Notwithstanding paragraph (1), a consumer reporting agency may terminate a reinvestigation of information disputed by a consumer under that paragraph if the agency reasonably determines that the dispute by the consumer is frivolous or irrelevant, including by reason of a failure by a consumer to provide sufficient information to investigate the disputed information. (B) Notice of determination. Upon making any determination in accordance with subparagraph (A) that a dispute is frivolous or irrelevant, a consumer reporting agency shall notify the consumer of such determination not later than 5 business days after making such determination, by mail or, if authorized by the consumer for that purpose, by any other means available to the agency. (C)

Contents of notice. A notice under subparagraph (B) shall include (i) the reasons for the determination under subparagraph (A); and (ii) identification of any information required to investigate the disputed information, which may consist of a standardized form describing the general nature of such information. (4) Consideration of consumer information. In conducting any reinvestigation under paragraph (1) with respect to disputed information in the file of any consumer, the consumer reporting agency shall review and consider all relevant information submitted by the consumer in the period described in paragraph (1)(A) with respect to such disputed information. (5) Treatment of inaccurate or unverifiable information. (A) In general. If, after any reinvestigation under paragraph (1) of any information disputed by a consumer, an item of the information is found to be inaccurate or incomplete or cannot be verified, the consumer reporting agency shall promptly delete that item of information from the consumer's file or modify that item of information, as appropriate, based on the results of the reinvestigation. (B) Requirements relating to reinsertion of previously deleted material. (i) Certification of accuracy of information. If any information is deleted from a consumer's file pursuant to subparagraph (A), the information may not be reinserted in the file by the consumer reporting agency unless the person who furnishes the information certifies that the information is complete and accurate. (ii) Notice to consumer. If any information that has been deleted from a consumer's file pursuant to subparagraph (A) is reinserted in the file, the consumer reporting agency shall notify the consumer of the reinsertion in writing not later than 5 business days after the reinsertion or, if authorized by the consumer for that purpose, by any other means available to the agency. (iii) Additional information. As part of, or in addition to, the notice under clause (ii), a consumer reporting agency shall provide to a consumer in writing not later than 5 business days after the date of the reinsertion (I) a statement that the disputed information has been reinserted; (II) the business name and address of any furnisher of information contacted and the telephone number of such furnisher, if reasonably available, or of any furnisher of information that contacted the consumer reporting agency, in connection with the reinsertion of such information; and (III) a notice that the consumer has the right to add a statement to the consumer's file disputing the accuracy or completeness of the disputed information. (C) Procedures to prevent reappearance. A consumer reporting agency shall maintain reasonable procedures designed to prevent the reappearance in a consumer's file, and in consumer reports on the consumer, of information that is deleted pursuant to this paragraph (other than information that is reinserted in accordance with

The Guide to Identity Theft Prevention

subparagraph (B)(i)). (D) Automated reinvestigation system. Any consumer reporting agency that compiles and maintains files on consumers on a nationwide basis shall implement an automated system through which furnishers of information to that consumer reporting agency may report the results of a reinvestigation that finds incomplete or inaccurate information in a consumer's file to other such consumer reporting agencies. (6) Notice of results of reinvestigation. (A) In general. A consumer reporting agency shall provide written notice to a consumer of the results of a reinvestigation under this subsection not later than 5 business days after the completion of the reinvestigation, by mail or, if authorized by the consumer for that purpose, by other means available to the agency. (B) Contents. As part of, or in addition to, the notice under subparagraph (A), a consumer reporting agency shall provide to a consumer in writing before the expiration of the 5-day period referred to in subparagraph (A) (i) a statement that the reinvestigation is completed; (ii) a consumer report that is based upon the consumer's file as that file is revised as a result of the reinvestigation; (iii) a notice that, if requested by the consumer, a description of the procedure used to determine the accuracy and completeness of the information shall be provided to the consumer by the agency, including the business name and address of any furnisher of information contacted in connection with such information and the telephone number of such furnisher, if reasonably available; (iv) a notice that the consumer has the right to add a statement to the consumer's file disputing the accuracy or completeness of the information; and (v) a notice that the consumer has the right to request under subsection (d) that the consumer reporting agency furnish notifications under that subsection. (7) Description of reinvestigation procedure. A consumer reporting agency shall provide to a consumer a description referred to in paragraph (6)(B)(iii) by not later than 15 days after receiving a request from the consumer for that description. (8) Expedited dispute resolution. If a dispute regarding an item of information in a consumer's file at a consumer reporting agency is resolved in accordance with paragraph (5)(A) by the deletion of the disputed information by not later than 3 business days after the date on which the agency receives notice of the dispute from the consumer in accordance with paragraph (1)(A), then the agency shall not be required to comply with paragraphs (2), (6), and (7) with respect to that dispute if the agency (A) provides prompt notice of the deletion to the consumer by telephone; (B) includes in that notice, or in a written notice that accompanies a confirmation and consumer report provided in accordance with subparagraph (C), a statement of the consumer's right to request under subsection (d) that the agency furnish notifications under that subsection; and (C) provides written confirmation of the deletion and a copy of a consumer report on the consumer that is based on the consumer's file after the deletion, not later than 5 business days after making the deletion. (b) Statement of dispute. If the reinvestigation does not resolve the dispute, the consumer may file a brief statement setting forth the nature of the dispute. The consumer reporting agency may limit such statements to not more than one hundred words if it provides the consumer with assistance in writing a clear summary of the dispute. (c) Notification of consumer dispute in subsequent consumer reports. Whenever a statement of a dispute is filed, unless there is reasonable grounds to believe that it is frivolous or irrelevant, the consumer reporting agency shall, in any subsequent consumer report containing the information in question, clearly note that it is disputed by the consumer and provide either the consumer's statement or a clear and accurate codification or summary thereof. (d) Notification of deletion of disputed information. Following any deletion of information which is found to be inaccurate or whose accuracy can no longer be verified or any notation as to disputed information, the consumer reporting agency shall, at the request of the consumer, furnish notification that the item has been deleted or the statement, codification or summary pursuant to subsection (b) or (c) of this section to any person specifically designated by the consumer who has within two years prior thereto received a consumer report for employment purposes, or within six months prior thereto received a consumer report for any other purpose, which contained the deleted or disputed information. **' 612. Charges for certain disclosures** [15 U.S.C. ' 1681j] (a) Reasonable charges allowed for certain disclosures. (1) In general. Except as provided in subsections (b), (c), and (d), a consumer reporting agency may impose a reasonable charge on a consumer (A) for making a disclosure to the consumer pursuant to section 609 [' 1681g], which charge (i) shall not exceed $8; and (ii) shall be indicated to the consumer before making the disclosure; and (B) for furnishing, pursuant to 611(d) [' 1681i], following a reinvestigation under section 611(a) [' 1681i], a statement, codification, or summary to a person designated by the consumer under that section after the 30-day period beginning on the date of notification of the consumer under paragraph (6) or (8) of section 611(a) [' 1681i] with respect to the reinvestigation, which charge (i) shall not exceed the charge that the agency would impose on each designated recipient for a consumer report; and (ii) shall be indicated to the consumer before furnishing such information. (2) Modification of amount. The Federal Trade Commission shall increase the amount referred to in paragraph (1)(A)(I) on January 1 of each year, based proportionally on changes in

The Guide to Identity Theft Prevention

the Consumer Price Index, with fractional changes rounded to the nearest fifty cents. (b) Free disclosure after adverse notice to consumer. Each consumer reporting agency that maintains a file on a consumer shall make all disclosures pursuant to section 609 [' 1681g] without charge to the consumer if, not later than 60 days after receipt by such consumer of a notification pursuant to section 615 [' 1681m], or of a notification from a debt collection agency affiliated with that consumer reporting agency stating that the consumer's credit rating may be or has been adversely affected, the consumer makes a request under section 609 [' 1681g]. (c) Free disclosure under certain other circumstances. Upon the request of the consumer, a consumer reporting agency shall make all disclosures pursuant to section 609 [' 1681g] once during any 12-month period without charge to that consumer if the consumer certifies in writing that the consumer (1) is unemployed and intends to apply for employment in the 60-day period beginning on the date on which the certification is made; (2) is a recipient of public welfare assistance; or (3) has reason to believe that the file on the consumer at the agency contains inaccurate information due to fraud. (d) Other charges prohibited. A consumer reporting agency shall not impose any charge on a consumer for providing any notification required by this title or making any disclosure required by this title, except as authorized by subsection (a). ' **613. Public record information for employment purposes** [15 U.S.C. ' 1681k] (a) In general. A consumer reporting agency which furnishes a consumer report for employment purposes and which for that purpose compiles and reports items of information on consumers which are matters of public record and are likely to have an adverse effect upon a consumer's ability to obtain employment shall (1) at the time such public record information is reported to the user of such consumer report, notify the consumer of the fact that public record information is being reported by the consumer reporting agency, together with the name and address of the person to whom such information is being reported; or (2) maintain strict procedures designed to insure that whenever public record information which is likely to have an adverse effect on a consumer's ability to obtain employment is reported it is complete and up to date. For purposes of this paragraph, items of public record relating to arrests, indictments, convictions, suits, tax liens, and outstanding judgments shall be considered up to date if the current public record status of the item at the time of the report is reported. (b) Exemption for national security investigations. Subsection (a) does not apply in the case of an agency or department of the United States Government that seeks to obtain and use a consumer report for employment purposes, if the head of the agency or department makes a written finding as prescribed under section 604(b)(4)(A). ' **614. Restrictions on investigative consumer reports** [15 U.S.C. ' 1681l] Whenever a consumer reporting agency prepares an investigative consumer report, no adverse information in the consumer report (other than information which is a matter of public record) may be included in a subsequent consumer report unless such adverse information has been verified in the process of making such subsequent consumer report, or the adverse information was received within the three-month period preceding the date the subsequent report is furnished. ' **615. Requirements on users of consumer reports** [15 U.S.C. ' 1681m] (a) Duties of users taking adverse actions on the basis of information contained in consumer reports. If any person takes any adverse action with respect to any consumer that is based in whole or in part on any information contained in a consumer report, the person shall (1) provide oral, written, or electronic notice of the adverse action to the consumer; (2) provide to the consumer orally, in writing, or electronically (A) the name, address, and telephone number of the consumer reporting agency (including a toll-free telephone number established by the agency if the agency compiles and maintains files on consumers on a nationwide basis) that furnished the report to the person; and (B) a statement that the consumer reporting agency did not make the decision to take the adverse action and is unable to provide the consumer the specific reasons why the adverse action was taken; and (3) provide to the consumer an oral, written, or electronic notice of the consumer's right (A) to obtain, under section 612 [' 1681j], a free copy of a consumer report on the consumer from the consumer reporting agency referred to in paragraph (2), which notice shall include an indication of the 60-day period under that section for obtaining such a copy; and (B) to dispute, under section 611 [' 1681i], with a consumer reporting agency the accuracy or completeness of any information in a consumer report furnished by the agency. (b) Adverse action based on information obtained from third parties other than consumer reporting agencies. (1) In general. Whenever credit for personal, family, or household purposes involving a consumer is denied or the charge for such credit is increased either wholly or partly because of information obtained from a person other than a consumer reporting agency bearing upon the consumer's credit worthiness, credit standing, credit capacity, character, general reputation, personal characteristics, or mode of living, the user of such information shall, within a reasonable period of time, upon the consumer's written request for the reasons for such adverse action received within sixty days after learning of such adverse action, disclose the nature of the information to the consumer. The user of such information shall clearly and

The Guide to Identity Theft Prevention

accurately disclose to the consumer his right to make such written request at the time such adverse action is communicated to the consumer. (2) Duties of person taking certain actions based on information provided by affiliate. (A) Duties, generally. If a person takes an action described in subparagraph (B) with respect to a consumer, based in whole or in part on information described in subparagraph (C), the person shall (i) notify the consumer of the action, including a statement that the consumer may obtain the information in accordance with clause (ii); and (ii) upon a written request from the consumer received within 60 days after transmittal of the notice required by clause (I), disclose to the consumer the nature of the information upon which the action is based by not later than 30 days after receipt of the request. (B) Action described. An action referred to in subparagraph (A) is an adverse action described in section 603(k)(1)(A) [' 1681a], taken in connection with a transaction initiated by the consumer, or any adverse action described in clause (i) or (ii) of section 603(k)(1)(B) [' 1681a]. (C) Information described. Information referred to in subparagraph (A) (i) except as provided in clause (ii), is information that (I) is furnished to the person taking the action by a person related by common ownership or affiliated by common corporate control to the person taking the action; and (II) bears on the credit worthiness, credit standing, credit capacity, character, general reputation, personal characteristics, or mode of living of the consumer; and (ii) does not include (I) information solely as to transactions or experiences between the consumer and the person furnishing the information; or (II) information in a consumer report. (c) Reasonable procedures to assure compliance. No person shall be held liable for any violation of this section if he shows by a preponderance of the evidence that at the time of the alleged violation he maintained reasonable procedures to assure compliance with the provisions of this section. (d) Duties of users making written credit or insurance solicitations on the basis of information contained in consumer files. (1) In general. Any person who uses a consumer report on any consumer in connection with any credit or insurance transaction that is not initiated by the consumer, that is provided to that person under section 604(c)(1)(B) [' 1681b], shall provide with each written solicitation made to the consumer regarding the transaction a clear and conspicuous statement that (A) information contained in the consumer's consumer report was used in connection with the transaction; (B) the consumer received the offer of credit or insurance because the consumer satisfied the criteria for credit worthiness or insurability under which the consumer was selected for the offer; (C) if applicable, the credit or insurance may not be extended if, after the consumer responds to the offer, the consumer does not meet the criteria used to select the consumer for the offer or any applicable criteria bearing on credit worthiness or insurability or does not furnish any required collateral; (D) the consumer has a right to prohibit information contained in the consumer's file with any consumer reporting agency from being used in connection with any credit or insurance transaction that is not initiated by the consumer; and (E) the consumer may exercise the right referred to in subparagraph (D) by notifying a notification system established under section 604(e) [' 1681b]. (2) Disclosure of address and telephone number. A statement under paragraph (1) shall include the address and toll-free telephone number of the appropriate notification system established under section 604(e) [' 1681b]. (3) Maintaining criteria on file. A person who makes an offer of credit or insurance to a consumer under a credit or insurance transaction described in paragraph (1) shall maintain on file the criteria used to select the consumer to receive the offer, all criteria bearing on credit worthiness or insurability, as applicable, that are the basis for determining whether or not to extend credit or insurance pursuant to the offer, and any requirement for the furnishing of collateral as a condition of the extension of credit or insurance, until the expiration of the 3-year period beginning on the date on which the offer is made to the consumer. (4) Authority of federal agencies regarding unfair or deceptive acts or practices not affected. This section is not intended to affect the authority of any Federal or State agency to enforce a prohibition against unfair or deceptive acts or practices, including the making of false or misleading statements in connection with a credit or insurance transaction that is not initiated by the consumer. **' 616. Civil liability for willful noncompliance** [15 U.S.C. ' 1681n] (a) In general. Any person who willfully fails to comply with any requirement imposed under this title with respect to any consumer is liable to that consumer in an amount equal to the sum of (1) (A) any actual damages sustained by the consumer as a result of the failure or damages of not less than $100 and not more than $1,000; or (B) in the case of liability of a natural person for obtaining a consumer report under false pretenses or knowingly without a permissible purpose, actual damages sustained by the consumer as a result of the failure or $1,000, whichever is greater; (2) such amount of punitive damages as the court may allow; and (3) in the case of any successful action to enforce any liability under this section, the costs of the action together with reasonable attorney's fees as determined by the court. (b) Civil liability for knowing noncompliance. Any person who obtains a consumer report from a consumer reporting agency under false pretenses or knowingly without a permissible purpose shall be liable to the consumer reporting agency for actual damages sustained by the consumer reporting agency or $1,000, whichever is greater. (c) Attorney's fees. Upon a finding by the court that an unsuccessful pleading, motion, or other paper filed in connection with an action under this section was filed in bad faith or for purposes of harassment, the court shall award to the prevailing party attorney's fees reasonable in relation to the work expended in responding to the pleading, motion, or other paper. ' **617. Civil liability for negligent noncompliance** [15 U.S.C. ' 1681o] (a) In general. Any person who is negligent in failing to comply with any requirement imposed under this title with respect to any consumer is liable to that consumer in an amount equal to the sum of (1) any actual damages sustained by the consumer as a result of the failure; (2) in the case of any successful action to enforce any liability under this section, the costs of the action together with reasonable attorney's fees as determined by the court. (b) Attorney's fees. On a finding by the court that an unsuccessful pleading, motion, or other paper filed in connection with an action under this section was filed in bad faith or for purposes of harassment, the court shall award to the prevailing party attorney's fees reasonable in relation to the work expended in responding to the pleading, motion, or other paper. ' **618. Jurisdiction of courts; limitation of actions** [15 U.S.C. ' 1681p] An action to enforce any liability created under this title may be brought in any appropriate United States district court without regard to the amount in controversy, or in any other court of competent jurisdiction, within two years from the date on which the liability arises, except that where a defendant has materially and willfully misrepresented any information required under this title to be disclosed to an individual and the information so misrepresented is material to the establishment of the defendant's liability to that individual under this title, the action may be brought at any time within two years after discovery by the individual of the misrepresentation. ' **619. Obtaining information under false pretenses** [15 U.S.C. ' 1681q] Any person who knowingly and willfully obtains information on a consumer from a consumer reporting agency under false pretenses shall be fined under title 18, United States Code, imprisoned for not more than 2 years, or both. ' **620. Unauthorized disclosures by officers or employees** [15 U.S.C. ' 1681r] Any officer or employee of a consumer reporting agency who knowingly and willfully provides information concerning an individual from the agency's files to a person not authorized to receive that information shall be fined under title 18, United States Code, imprisoned for not more than 2 years, or both. ' **621. Administrative enforcement** [15 U.S.C. ' 1681s] (a) (1) Enforcement by Federal Trade Commission. Compliance with the requirements imposed under this title shall be enforced under the Federal Trade Commission Act [15

Johnny R. May

U.S.C. " 41 et seq.] by the Federal Trade Commission with respect to consumer reporting agencies and all other persons subject thereto, except to the extent that enforcement of the requirements imposed under this title is specifically committed to some other government agency under subsection (b) hereof. For the purpose of the exercise by the Federal Trade Commission of its functions and powers under the Federal Trade Commission Act, a violation of any requirement or prohibition imposed under this title shall constitute an unfair or deceptive act or practice in commerce in violation of section 5(a) of the Federal Trade Commission Act [15 U.S.C. ' 45(a)] and shall be subject to enforcement by the Federal Trade Commission under section 5(b) thereof [15 U.S.C. ' 45(b)] with respect to any consumer reporting agency or person subject to enforcement by the Federal Trade Commission pursuant to this subsection, irrespective of whether that person is engaged in commerce or meets any other jurisdictional tests in the Federal Trade Commission Act. The Federal Trade Commission shall have such procedural, investigative, and enforcement powers, including the power to issue procedural rules in enforcing compliance with the requirements imposed under this title and to require the filing of reports, the production of documents, and the appearance of witnesses as though the applicable terms and conditions of the Federal Trade Commission Act were part of this title. Any person violating any of the provisions of this title shall be subject to the penalties and entitled to the privileges and immunities provided in the Federal Trade Commission Act as though the applicable terms and provisions thereof were part of this title. 2) (A) In the event of a knowing violation, which constitutes a pattern or practice of violations of this title, the Commission may commence a civil action to recover a civil penalty in a district court of the United States against any person that violates this title. In such action, such person shall be liable for a civil penalty of not more than $2,500 per violation. (B) In determining the amount of a civil penalty under subparagraph (A), the court shall take into account the degree of culpability, any history of prior such conduct, ability to pay, effect on ability to continue to do business, and such other matters as justice may require. (3) Notwithstanding paragraph (2), a court may not impose any civil penalty on a person for a violation of section 623(a)(1) [' 1681s-2] unless the person has been enjoined from committing the violation, or ordered not to commit the violation, in an action or proceeding brought by or on behalf of the Federal Trade Commission, and has violated the injunction or order, and the court may not impose any civil penalty for any violation occurring before the date of the violation of the injunction or order. (4) Neither the Commission nor any other agency referred to in subsection (b) may

The Guide to Identity Theft Prevention

prescribe trade regulation rules or other regulations with respect to this title. (b) Enforcement by other agencies. Compliance with the requirements imposed under this title with respect to consumer reporting agencies, persons who use consumer reports from such agencies, persons who furnish information to such agencies, and users of information that are subject to subsection (d) of section 615 [' 1681m] shall be enforced under (1) section 8 of the Federal Deposit Insurance Act [12 U.S.C. ' 1818], in the case of (A) national banks, and Federal branches and Federal agencies of foreign banks, by the Office of the Comptroller of the Currency; (B) member banks of the Federal Reserve System (other than national banks), branches and agencies of foreign banks (other than Federal branches, Federal agencies, and insured State branches of foreign banks), commercial lending companies owned or controlled by foreign banks, and organizations operating under section 25 or 25(a) [25A] of the Federal Reserve Act [12 U.S.C. " 601 et seq., " 611 et seq], by the Board of Governors of the Federal Reserve System; and (C) banks insured by the Federal Deposit Insurance Corporation (other than members of the Federal Reserve System) and insured State branches of foreign banks, by the Board of Directors of the Federal Deposit Insurance Corporation; (2) section 8 of the Federal Deposit Insurance Act [12 U.S.C. ' 1818], by the Director of the Office of Thrift Supervision, in the case of a savings association the deposits of which are insured by the Federal Deposit Insurance Corporation; (3) the Federal Credit Union Act [12 U.S.C. " 1751 et seq.], by the Administrator of the National Credit Union Administration [National Credit Union Administration Board] with respect to any Federal credit union; (4) subtitle IV of title 49 [49 U.S.C. " 10101 et seq.], by the Secretary of Transportation, with respect to all carriers subject to the jurisdiction of the Surface Transportation Board; (5) the Federal Aviation Act of 1958 [49 U.S.C. Appx " 1301 et seq.], by the Secretary of Transportation with respect to any air carrier or foreign air carrier subject to that Act [49 U.S.C. Appx " 1301 et seq.]; and (6) the Packers and Stockyards Act, 1921 [7 U.S.C. " 181 et seq.] (except as provided in section 406 of that Act [7 U.S.C. " 226 and 227]), by the Secretary of Agriculture with respect to any activities subject to that Act. The terms used in paragraph (1) that are not defined in this title or otherwise defined in section 3(s) of the Federal Deposit Insurance Act (12 U.S.C. ' 1813(s)) shall have the meaning given to them in section 1(b) of the International Banking Act of 1978 (12 U.S.C. ' 3101). (c) State action for violations. (1) Authority of states. In addition to such other remedies as are provided under State law, if the chief law enforcement officer of a State, or an official or agency designated by a State, has reason to believe that any person has

Johnny R. May

violated or is violating this title, the State (A) may bring an action to enjoin such violation in any appropriate United States district court or in any other court of competent jurisdiction; (B) subject to paragraph (5), may bring an action on behalf of the residents of the State to recover (i) damages for which the person is liable to such residents under sections 616 and 617 [" 1681n and 1681o] as a result of the violation; (ii) in the case of a violation of section 623(a) [' 1681s-2], damages for which the person would, but for section 623(c) [' 1681s-2], be liable to such residents as a result of the violation; or (iii) damages of not more than $1,000 for each willful or negligent violation; and (C) in the case of any successful action under subparagraph (A) or (B), shall be awarded the costs of the action and reasonable attorney fees as determined by the court. (2) Rights of federal regulators. The State shall serve prior written notice of any action under paragraph (1) upon the Federal Trade Commission or the appropriate Federal regulator determined under subsection (b) and provide the Commission or appropriate Federal regulator with a copy of its complaint, except in any case in which such prior notice is not feasible, in which case the State shall serve such notice immediately upon instituting such action. The Federal Trade Commission or appropriate Federal regulator shall have the right (A) to intervene in the action; (B) upon so intervening, to be heard on all matters arising therein; (C) to remove the action to the appropriate United States district court; and (D) to file petitions for appeal. (3) Investigatory powers. For purposes of bringing any action under this subsection, nothing in this subsection shall prevent the chief law enforcement officer, or an official or agency designated by a State, from exercising the powers conferred on the chief law enforcement officer or such official by the laws of such State to conduct investigations or to administer oaths or affirmations or to compel the attendance of witnesses or the production of documentary and other evidence. (4) Limitation on state action while federal action pending. If the Federal Trade Commission or the appropriate Federal regulator has instituted a civil action or an administrative action under section 8 of the Federal Deposit Insurance Act for a violation of this title, no State may, during the pendency of such action, bring an action under this section against any defendant named in the complaint of the Commission or the appropriate Federal regulator for any violation of this title that is alleged in that complaint. (5) Limitations on state actions for violation of section 623(a)(1) [' 1681s-2]. (A) Violation of injunction required. A State may not bring an action against a person under paragraph (1)(B) for a violation of section 623(a)(1) [' 1681s-2], unless (i) the person has been enjoined from committing the violation, in an action brought by the State under paragraph (1)(A); and (ii) the person has violated the injunction. (B) Limitation on damages recoverable. In an action against a person under paragraph (1)(B) for a violation of section 623(a)(1) [' 1681s-2], a State may not recover any damages incurred before the date of the violation of an injunction on which the action is based. (d) Enforcement under other authority. For the purpose of the exercise by any agency referred to in subsection (b) of this section of its powers under any Act referred to in that subsection, a violation of any requirement imposed under this title shall be deemed to be a violation of a requirement imposed under that Act. In addition to its powers under any provision of law specifically referred to in subsection (b) of this section, each of the agencies referred to in that subsection may exercise, for the purpose of enforcing compliance with any requirement imposed under this title any other authority conferred on it by law. Notwithstanding the preceding, no agency referred to in subsection (b) may conduct an examination of a bank, savings association, or credit union regarding compliance with the provisions of this title, except in response to a complaint (or if the agency otherwise has knowledge) that the bank, savings association, or credit union has violated a provision of this title, in which case, the agency may conduct an examination as necessary to investigate the complaint. If an agency determines during an investigation in response to a complaint that a violation of this title has occurred, the agency may, during its next 2 regularly scheduled examinations of the bank, savings association, or credit union, examine for compliance with this title. (e) Interpretive authority. The Board of Governors of the Federal Reserve System may issue interpretations of any provision of this title as such provision may apply to any persons identified under paragraph (1), (2), and (3) of subsection (b), or to the holding companies and affiliates of such persons, in consultation with Federal agencies identified in paragraphs (1), (2), and (3) of subsection (b). ' 622. **Information on overdue child support obligations** [15 U.S.C. ' 1681s-1] Notwithstanding any other provision of this title, a consumer reporting agency shall include in any consumer report furnished by the agency in accordance with section 604 [' 1681b] of this title, any information on the failure of the consumer to pay overdue support which (1) is provided (A) to the consumer reporting agency by a State or local child support enforcement agency; or (B) to the consumer reporting agency and verified by any local, State, or Federal government agency; and (2) antedates the report by 7 years or less. ' **623. Responsibilities of furnishers of information to consumer reporting agencies** [15 U.S.C. ' 1681s-2] (a) Duty of furnishers of information to provide accurate information. (1) Prohibition. (A) Reporting information with actual knowledge of errors. A person shall not furnish any information relating to a consumer to any consumer reporting agency if the person knows or consciously avoids knowing that the information is inaccurate. (B) Reporting information after notice and confirmation of errors. A person shall not furnish information relating to a consumer to any consumer reporting agency if (i) the person has been notified by the consumer, at the address specified by the person for such notices, that specific information is inaccurate; and (ii) the information is, in fact, inaccurate. (C) No address requirement. A person who clearly and conspicuously specifies to the consumer an address for notices referred to in subparagraph (B) shall not be subject to subparagraph (A); however, nothing in subparagraph (B) shall require a person to specify such an address. (2) Duty to correct and update information. A person who (A) regularly and in the ordinary course of business furnishes information to one or more consumer reporting agencies about the person's transactions or experiences with any consumer; and (B) has furnished to a consumer reporting agency information that the person determines is not complete or accurate, shall promptly notify the consumer reporting agency of that determination and provide to the agency any corrections to that information, or any additional information, that is necessary to make the information provided by the person to the agency complete and accurate, and shall not thereafter furnish to the agency any of the information that remains not complete or accurate. (3) Duty to provide notice of dispute. If the completeness or accuracy of any information furnished by any person to any consumer reporting agency is disputed to such person by a consumer, the person may not furnish the information to any consumer reporting agency without notice that such information is disputed by the consumer. (4) Duty to provide notice of closed accounts. A person who regularly and in the ordinary course of business furnishes information to a consumer reporting agency regarding a consumer who has a credit account with that person shall notify the agency of the voluntary closure of the account by the consumer, in information regularly furnished for the period in which the account is closed. (5) Duty to provide notice of delinquency of accounts. A person who furnishes information to a consumer reporting agency regarding a delinquent account being placed for collection, charged to profit or loss, or subjected to any similar action shall, not later than 90 days after furnishing the information, notify the agency of the month and year of the commencement of the delinquency that immediately preceded the action. (b) Duties of furnishers of information upon notice of dispute. (1) In general. After receiving notice pursuant to section 611(a)(2) [' 1681i] of a dispute with regard to the completeness or accuracy of any information provided by a person to a consumer reporting agency, the person shall (A) conduct an investigation with respect to the disputed information; (B) review all relevant information provided by the consumer reporting agency pursuant to section 611(a)(2) [' 1681i]; (C) report the results of the investigation to the consumer reporting agency; and (D) if the investigation finds that the information is incomplete or inaccurate, report those results to all other consumer reporting agencies to which the person furnished the information and that compile and maintain files on consumers on a nationwide basis. (2) Deadline. A person shall complete all investigations, reviews, and reports required under paragraph (1) regarding information provided by the person to a consumer reporting agency, before the expiration of the period under section 611(a)(1) [' 1681i] within which the consumer reporting agency is required to complete actions required by that section regarding that information. (c) Limitation on liability. Sections 616 and 617 [" 1681n and 1681o] do not apply to any failure to comply with subsection (a), except as provided in section 621(c)(1)(B) [' 1681s]. (d) Limitation on enforcement. Subsection (a) shall be enforced exclusively under section 621 [' 1681s] by the Federal agencies and officials and the State officials identified in that section. ' **624. Relation to State laws** [15 U.S.C. ' 1681t] (a) In general. Except as provided in subsections (b) and (c), this title does not annul, alter, affect, or exempt any person subject to the provisions of this title from complying with the laws of any State with respect to the collection, distribution, or use of any information on consumers, except to the extent that those laws are inconsistent with any provision of this title, and then only to the extent of the inconsistency. (b) General exceptions. No requirement or prohibition may be imposed under the laws of any State (1) with respect to any subject matter regulated under (A) subsection (c) or (e) of section 604 [' 1681b], relating to the prescreening of consumer reports; (B) section 611 [' 1681i], relating to the time by which a consumer reporting agency must take any action, including the provision of notification to a consumer or other person, in any procedure related to the disputed accuracy of information in a consumer's file, except that this subparagraph shall not apply to any State law in effect on the date of enactment of the Consumer Credit Reporting Reform Act of 1996; (C) subsections (a) and (b) of section 615 [' 1681m], relating to the duties of a person who takes any adverse action with respect to a consumer; (D) section 615(d) [' 1681m], relating to the duties of persons who use a consumer report of a consumer in connection with any credit or insurance transaction that is not initiated by the consumer and that consists of a firm offer of credit or insurance; (E) section 605 [' 1681c], relating to information contained in consumer reports, except that this subparagraph shall not apply to any State law in effect on the date of enactment of the Consumer Credit Reporting Reform Act of 1996; or (F) section 623 [' 1681s-2], relating to the responsibilities of persons who furnish information to consumer reporting agencies, except that this paragraph shall not apply (i) with respect to section 54A(a) of chapter 93 of the Massachusetts Annotated Laws (as in effect on the date of enactment of the Consumer Credit Reporting Reform Act of 1996); or (ii) with respect to section 1785.25(a) of the California Civil Code (as in effect on the date of enactment of the Consumer Credit Reporting Reform Act of 1996); (2) with respect to the exchange of information among persons affiliated by common ownership or common corporate control, except that this paragraph shall not apply with respect to subsection (a) or (c)(1) of section 2480e of title 9, Vermont Statutes Annotated (as in effect on the date of enactment of the Consumer Credit Reporting Reform Act of 1996); or (3) with respect to the form and content of any disclosure required to be made under section 609(c) [' 1681g]. (c) Definition of firm offer of credit or insurance. Notwithstanding any definition of the term "firm offer of credit or insurance" (or any equivalent term) under the laws of any State, the definition of that term contained in section 603(l) [' 1681a] shall be construed to apply in the enforcement and interpretation of the laws of any State governing consumer reports. (d) Limitations. Subsections (b) and (c) (1) do not affect any settlement, agreement, or consent judgment between any State Attorney General and any consumer reporting agency in effect on the date of enactment of the Consumer Credit Reporting Reform Act of 1996; and (2) do not apply to any provision of State law (including any provision of a State constitution) that (A) is enacted after January 1, 2004; (B) states explicitly that the provision is intended to supplement this title; and (C) gives greater protection to consumers than is provided under this title. '

625. Disclosures to FBI for counterintelligence purposes [15 U.S.C. ' 1681u] (a) Identity of financial institutions. Notwithstanding section 604 [' 1681b] or any other provision of this title, a consumer reporting agency shall furnish to the Federal Bureau of Investigation the names and addresses of all financial institutions (as that term is defined in section 1101 of the Right to Financial Privacy Act of 1978 [12 U.S.C. ' 3401]) at which a consumer maintains or has maintained an account, to the extent that information is in the files of the agency, when presented with a written request for that information, signed by the Director of the Federal Bureau of Investigation, or the Director's designee, which certifies compliance with this section. The Director or the Director's designee may make such a certification only if the Director or the Director's designee has determined in writing that (1) such information

The Guide to Identity Theft Prevention

is necessary for the conduct of an authorized foreign counterintelligence investigation; and (2) there are specific and articulable facts giving reason to believe that the consumer (A) is a foreign power (as defined in section 101 of the Foreign Intelligence Surveillance Act of 1978 [50 U.S.C. ' 1801]) or a person who is not a United States person (as defined in such section 101) and is an official of a foreign power; or (B) is an agent of a foreign power and is engaging or has engaged in an act of international terrorism (as that term is defined in section 101(c) of the Foreign Intelligence Surveillance Act of 1978 [50 U.S.C. ' 1801(c)]) or clandestine intelligence activities that involve or may involve a violation of criminal statutes of the United States. (b) Identifying information. Notwithstanding the provisions of section 604 [' 1681b] or any other provision of this title, a consumer reporting agency shall furnish identifying information respecting a consumer, limited to name, address, former addresses, places of employment, or former places of employment, to the Federal Bureau of Investigation when presented with a written request, signed by the Director or the Director's designee, which certifies compliance with this subsection. The Director or the Director's designee may make such a certification only if the Director or the Director's designee has determined in writing that (1) such information is necessary to the conduct of an authorized counterintelligence investigation; and (2) there is information giving reason to believe that the consumer has been, or is about to be, in contact with a foreign power or an agent of a foreign power (as defined in section 101 of the Foreign Intelligence Surveillance Act of 1978 [50 U.S.C. ' 1801]). (c) Court order for disclosure of consumer reports. Notwithstanding section 604 [' 1681b] or any other provision of this title, if requested in writing by the Director of the Federal Bureau of Investigation, or a designee of the Director, a court may issue an order ex parte directing a consumer reporting agency to furnish a consumer report to the Federal Bureau of Investigation, upon a showing in camera that (1) the consumer report is necessary for the conduct of an authorized foreign counterintelligence investigation; and (2) there are specific and articulable facts giving reason to believe that the consumer whose consumer report is sought (A) is an agent of a foreign power, and (B) is engaging or has engaged in an act of international terrorism (as that term is defined in section 101(c) of the Foreign Intelligence Surveillance Act of 1978 [50 U.S.C. ' 1801(c)]) or clandestine intelligence activities that involve or may involve a violation of criminal statutes of the United States. The terms of an order issued under this subsection shall not disclose that the order is issued for purposes of a counterintelligence investigation. (d) Confidentiality. No consumer reporting agency or officer, employee, or agent of a consumer reporting agency shall disclose to any person, other than those officers, employees, or agents of a consumer reporting agency necessary to fulfill the requirement to disclose information to the Federal Bureau of Investigation under this section, that the Federal Bureau of Investigation has sought or obtained the identity of financial institutions or a consumer report respecting any consumer under subsection (a), (b), or (c), and no consumer reporting agency or officer, employee, or agent of a consumer reporting agency shall include in any consumer report any information that would indicate that the Federal Bureau of Investigation has sought or obtained such information or a consumer report. (e) Payment of fees. The Federal Bureau of Investigation shall, subject to the availability of appropriations, pay to the consumer reporting agency assembling or providing report or information in accordance with procedures established under this section a fee for reimbursement for such costs as are reasonably necessary and which have been directly incurred in searching, reproducing, or transporting books, papers, records, or other data required or requested to be produced under this section. (f) Limit on dissemination. The Federal Bureau of Investigation may not disseminate information obtained pursuant to this section outside of the Federal Bureau of Investigation, except to other Federal agencies as may be necessary for the approval or conduct of a foreign counterintelligence investigation, or, where the information concerns a person subject to the Uniform Code of Military Justice, to appropriate investigative authorities within the military department concerned as may be necessary for the conduct of a joint foreign counterintelligence investigation. (g) Rules of construction. Nothing in this section shall be construed to prohibit information from being furnished by the Federal Bureau of Investigation pursuant to a subpoena or court order, in connection with a judicial or administrative proceeding to enforce the provisions of this Act. Nothing in this section shall be construed to authorize or permit the withholding of information from the Congress. (h) Reports to Congress. On a semiannual basis, the Attorney General shall fully inform the Permanent Select Committee on Intelligence and the Committee on Banking, Finance and Urban Affairs of the House of Representatives, and the Select Committee on Intelligence and the Committee on Banking, Housing, and Urban Affairs of the Senate concerning all requests made pursuant to subsections (a), (b), and (c). (i) Damages. Any agency or department of the United States obtaining or disclosing any consumer reports, records, or information contained therein in violation of this section is liable to the consumer to whom such consumer reports, records, or information relate in an amount

The Guide to Identity Theft Prevention

equal to the sum of (1) $100, without regard to the volume of consumer reports, records, or information involved; (2) any actual damages sustained by the consumer as a result of the disclosure; (3) if the violation is found to have been willful or intentional, such punitive damages as a court may allow; and (4) in the case of any successful action to enforce liability under this subsection, the costs of the action, together with reasonable attorney fees, as determined by the court. (j) Disciplinary actions for violations. If a court determines that any agency or department of the United States has violated any provision of this section and the court finds that the circumstances surrounding the violation raise questions of whether or not an officer or employee of the agency or department acted willfully or intentionally with respect to the violation, the agency or department shall promptly initiate a proceeding to determine whether or not disciplinary action is warranted against the officer or employee who was responsible for the violation. (k) Good-faith exception. Notwithstanding any other provision of this title, any consumer reporting agency or agent or employee thereof making disclosure of consumer reports or identifying information pursuant to this subsection in good-faith reliance upon a certification of the Federal Bureau of Investigation pursuant to provisions of this section shall not be liable to any person for such disclosure under this title, the constitution of any State, or any law or regulation of any State or any political subdivision of any State. (l) Limitation of remedies. Notwithstanding any other provision of this title, the remedies and sanctions set forth in this section shall be the only judicial remedies and sanctions for violation of this section. (m) Injunctive relief. In addition to any other remedy contained in this section, injunctive relief shall be available to require compliance with the procedures of this section. In the event of any successful action under this subsection, costs together with reasonable attorney fees, as determined by the court, may be recovered. **Legislative History House Reports: No. 91-975 (Comm. on Banking and Currency) and No. 91-1587 (Comm. of Conference) Senate Reports: No. 91-1139 accompanying S. 3678 (Comm. on Banking and Currency) Congressional Record, Vol. 116 (1970) May 25, considered and passed House. Sept. 18, considered and passed Senate, amended. Oct. 9, Senate agreed to conference report. Oct. 13, House agreed to conference report. Enactment: Public Law No. 91-508 (October 26, 1970): Amendments: Public Law Nos. 95-473 (October 17, 1978) 95-598 (November 6, 1978) 98-443 (October 4, 1984) 101-73 (August 9, 1989) 102-242 (December 19, 1991) 102-537 (October 27, 1992) 102-550 (October 28, 1992) 103-325 (September 23, 1994) 104-88 (December 29, 1995) 104-93 (January 6, 1996) 104-193 (August 22, 1996) 104-208 (September 30, 1996)**

105-107 (November 20, 1997) 105-347 (November 2, 1998) 1. The reporting periods have been lengthened for certain adverse information pertaining to U.S. Government insured or guaranteed student loans, or pertaining to national direct student loans. See sections 430A(f) and 463(c)(3) of the Higher Education Act of 1965, 20 U.S.C. 1080a(f) and 20 U.S.C. 1087cc(c)(3), respectively. ** Should read "paragraphs (4) and (5). ." Prior Section 605(a)(6) was amended and redesignated as Section 605(a)(5) in November 1998.

The Guide to Identity Theft Prevention

OK TO COPY THIS APPENDIX

Appendix I: Identity Theft and Assumption Deterrence Act

IDENTITY THEFT AND ASSUMPTION DETERRENCE ACT As amended by Public Law 105-318, 112 Stat. 3007 (Oct. 30, 1998) An Act To amend chapter 47 of title 18, United States Code, relating to identity theft, and for other purposes. [NOTE: Oct. 30, 1998 - [H.R. 4151] *Be it enacted by the Senate and House of Representatives of the United States of America in Congress assembled,* [NOTE: Identity Theft and Assumption Deterrence Act of 1998.] Sec. 001. Short Title 002. Constitutional Authority to Enact this Legislation. 003. Identity Theft 004. Amendment of Federal Sentencing Guidelines for Offenses Under Section 1028 005. Centralized Complaint and Consumer Education Service for Victims of Identity Theft 006. Technical Amendments to Title 18, United States Code 007. Redaction of Ethics Reports Filed by Judicial Officers and Employees ' **001. Short Title. [NOTE: 18 USC 1001 note.]** This Act may be cited as the "Identity Theft and Assumption Deterrence Act of 1998". ' **002. Constitutional Authority to Enact this Legislation. [NOTE: 18 USC 1028 note.]** The constitutional authority upon which this Act rests is the power of Congress to regulate commerce with foreign nations and among the several States, and the authority to make all laws which shall be necessary and proper for carrying into execution the powers vested by the Constitution in the Government of the United States or in any department or officer thereof, as set forth in article I, section 8 of the United States Constitution. ' **003. Identity Theft.** (a) Establishment of Offense.—Section 1028(a) of title 18, United States Code, is amended— (1) in paragraph (5), by striking "or" at the end; (2) in paragraph (6), by adding "or" at the end; (3) in the flush matter following paragraph (6), by striking "or attempts to do so,"; and (4) by inserting after paragraph (6) the following: "(7) knowingly transfers or uses, without lawful authority, a means of identification of another person with the intent to commit, or to aid or abet, any unlawful activity that constitutes a violation of Federal law, or that constitutes a felony under any applicable State or local law;". (b) Penalties.— Section 1028(b) of title 18, United States Code, is amended— (1) in paragraph (1)— (A) in subparagraph (B), by striking "or" at the end; (B) in subparagraph (C), by adding "or" at the end; and (C) by adding at the end the following: "(D) an offense under paragraph (7) of such subsection that involves the transfer or use of 1 or more means of identification if, as a result of the offense, any individual committing the offense obtains anything of value aggregating $1,000 or more during any 1-year period;"; (2) in paragraph (2)— (A) in subparagraph (A), by striking "or transfer of an identification document or" and inserting ", transfer, or use of a means of identification, an identification document, or a"; and (B) in subparagraph (B), by inserting "or (7)" after "(3)"; (3) by amending paragraph (3) to read as follows: "(3) a fine under this title or imprisonment for not more than 20 years, or both, if the offense is committed— "(A) to facilitate a drug trafficking crime (as defined in section 929(a)(2)); "(B) in connection with a crime of violence (as defined in section 924(c)(3)); or "(C) after a prior conviction under this section becomes final;"; (4) in paragraph (4), by striking "and" at the end; (5) by redesignating paragraph (5) as paragraph (6); and (6) by inserting after paragraph (4) the following: "(5) in the case of any offense under subsection (a), forfeiture to the United States of any personal property used or intended to be used to commit the offense; and". (c) Circumstances.—Section 1028(c) of title 18, United States Code, is amended by striking paragraph (3) and inserting the following: "(3) either— "(A) the production, transfer, possession, or use prohibited by this section is in or affects interstate or foreign commerce; or "(B) the means of identification, identification document, false identification document, or document- making implement is transported in the mail in the course of the production, transfer, possession, or use prohibited by this section.". (d) Definitions.—Subsection (d) of section 1028 of title 18, United States Code, is amended to read as follows: "(d) In this section— "(1) the term `document-making implement' means any implement, impression, electronic device, or computer hardware or software, that is specifically configured or primarily used for making an identification document, a false identification document, or another document-making implement; "(2) the term `identification document' means a document made or issued by or under the authority of the United States Government, a State, political subdivision of a State, a foreign government, political subdivision of a foreign government, an international governmental or

The Guide to Identity Theft Prevention

an international quasi-governmental organization which, when completed with information concerning a particular individual, is of a type intended or commonly accepted for the purpose of identification of individuals; "(3) the term `means of identification' means any name or number that may be used, alone or in conjunction with any other information, to identify a specific individual, including any— "(A) name, social security number, date of birth, official State or government issued driver's license or identification number, alien registration number, government passport number, employer or taxpayer identification number; "(B) unique biometric data, such as fingerprint, voice print, retina or iris image, or other unique physical representation; "(C) unique electronic identification number, address, or routing code; or "(D) telecommunication identifying information or access device (as defined in section 1029(e)); "(4) the term `personal identification card' means an identification document issued by a State or local government solely for the purpose of identification; "(5) the term `produce' includes alter, authenticate, or assemble; and "(6) the term `State' includes any State of the United States, the District of Columbia, the Commonwealth of Puerto Rico, and any other commonwealth, possession, or territory of the United States.". (e) Attempt and Conspiracy.—Section 1028 of title 18, United States Code, is amended by adding at the end the following: "(f) Attempt and Conspiracy.—Any person who attempts or conspires to commit any offense under this section shall be subject to the same penalties as those prescribed for the offense, the commission of which was the object of the attempt or conspiracy.". (f) Forfeiture Procedures.—Section 1028 of title 18, United States Code, is amended by adding at the end the following: "(g) Forfeiture Procedures.—The forfeiture of property under this section, including any seizure and disposition of the property and any related judicial or administrative proceeding, shall be governed by the provisions of section 413 (other than subsection (d) of that section) of the Comprehensive Drug Abuse Prevention and Control Act of 1970 (21 U.S.C. 853).". (g) Rule of Construction.—Section 1028 of title 18, United States Code, is amended by adding at the end the following: "(h) Rule of Construction.—For purpose of subsection (a)(7), a single identification document or false identification document that contains 1 or more means of identification shall be construed to be 1 means of identification.". (h) Conforming Amendments.—Chapter 47 of title 18, United States Code, is amended— (1) in the heading for section 1028, by adding "**and information**" at the end; and (2) in the table of sections at the beginning of the chapter, in the item relating to section 1028, by adding "and information" at the end. ' **004. Amendment of Federal Sentencing Guidelines for Offenses Under Section 1028. [NOTE: 28 USC 994 note.]** (a) In General.—Pursuant to its authority under section 994(p) of title 28, United States Code, the United States Sentencing Commission shall review and amend the Federal sentencing guidelines and the policy statements of the Commission, as appropriate, to provide an appropriate penalty for each offense under section 1028 of title 18, United States Code, as amended by this Act. (b) Factors for Consideration.—In carrying out subsection (a), the United States Sentencing Commission shall consider, with respect to each offense described in subsection (a)— (1) the extent to which the number of victims (as defined in section 3663A(a) of title 18, United States Code) involved in the offense, including harm to reputation, inconvenience, and other difficulties resulting from the offense, is an adequate measure for establishing penalties under the Federal sentencing guidelines; (2) the number of means of identification, identification documents, or false identification documents (as those terms are defined in section 1028(d) of title 18, United States Code, as amended by this Act) involved in the offense, is an adequate measure for establishing penalties under the Federal sentencing guidelines; (3) the extent to which the value of the loss to any individual caused by the offense is an adequate measure for establishing penalties under the Federal sentencing guidelines; (4) the range of conduct covered by the offense; (5) the extent to which sentencing enhancements within the Federal sentencing guidelines and the court's authority to sentence above the applicable guideline range are adequate to ensure punishment at or near the maximum penalty for the most egregious conduct covered by the offense; (6) the extent to which Federal sentencing guidelines sentences for the offense have been constrained by statutory maximum penalties; (7) the extent to which Federal sentencing guidelines for the offense adequately achieve the purposes of sentencing set forth in section 3553(a)(2) of title 18, United States Code; and (8) any other factor that the United States Sentencing Commission considers to be appropriate. ' **005. Centralized Complaing and Consumer Education Service for Victims of Identity Theft. [NOTE: 18 USC 1028 note.]** (a) In <<NOTE: Deadline.>> General.—Not later than 1 year after the date of enactment of this Act, the Federal Trade Commission shall establish procedures to— (1) log and acknowledge the receipt of complaints by

The Guide to Identity Theft Prevention

individuals who certify that they have a reasonable belief that 1 or more of their means of identification (as defined in section 1028 of title 18, United States Code, as amended by this Act) have been assumed, stolen, or otherwise unlawfully acquired in violation of section 1028 of title 18, United States Code, as amended by this Act; (2) provide informational materials to individuals described in paragraph (1); and (3) refer complaints described in paragraph (1) to appropriate entities, which may include referral to— (A) the 3 major national consumer reporting agencies; and (B) appropriate law enforcement agencies for potential law enforcement action. (b) Authorization of Appropriations.—There are authorized to be appropriated such sums as may be necessary to carry out this section. ' **006. Technical Amendments to Title 18, United States Code.** (a) Technical Correction Relating to Criminal Forfeiture Procedures.—Section 982(b)(1) of title 18, United States Code, is amended to read as follows: "(1) The forfeiture of property under this section, including any seizure and disposition of the property and any related judicial or administrative proceeding, shall be governed by the provisions of section 413 (other than subsection (d) of that section) of the Comprehensive Drug Abuse Prevention and Control Act of 1970 (21 U.S.C. 853).". (b) Economic Espionage and Theft of Trade Secrets as Predicate Offenses for Wire Interception.-Section 2516(1)(a) of title 18, United States Code, is amended by inserting "chapter 90 (relating to protection of trade secrets)," after "to espionage),". ' **007. Redaction of Ethics Reports Filed by Judicial Officers and Employees.** Section 105(b) of the Ethics in Government Act of 1978 (5 U.S.C. App.) is amended by adding at the end the following new paragraph: "(3)(A) This section does not require the immediate and unconditional availability of reports filed by an individual described in section 109(8) or 109(10) of this Act if a finding is made by the Judicial Conference, in consultation with United States Marshall Service, that revealing personal and sensitive information could endanger that individual. "(B) A report may be redacted pursuant to this paragraph only— "(i) to the extent necessary to protect the individual who filed the report; and "(ii) for as long as the danger to such individual exists. "(C) The Administrative Office of the United States Courts shall submit to the Committees on the Judiciary of the House of Representatives and of the Senate an annual report with respect to the operation of this paragraph including— "(i) the total number of reports redacted pursuant to this paragraph; "(ii) the total number of individuals whose reports have been redacted pursuant to this paragraph; and "(iii) the types of threats against individuals whose reports are redacted, if appropriate. "(D) The Judicial Conference, in consultation with the Department of Justice, shall issue regulations setting forth the circumstances under which redaction is appropriate under this paragraph and the procedures for redaction.[NOTE: Regulations.] "(E) This paragraph shall expire on December 31, 2001, and apply to filings through calendar year 2001.". [NOTE: Expiration date.] Approved October 30, 1998. **LEGISLATIVE HISTORY—H.R. 4151 (S. 512):** SENATE REPORTS: No. 105-274 accompanying S. 512 (Comm. on the Judiciary). CONGRESSIONAL RECORD, Vol. 144 (1998): Oct. 7, considered and passed House. Oct. 14, considered and passed Senate. WEEKLY COMPILATION OF PRESIDENTIAL DOCUMENTS, Vol. 34 (1998): Oct. 30, Presidential statement.

INDEX

Accounts, 98
ATM, 20, 24, 50, 55, 58
California Public Interest Group (CALPIRG), 7
calling card, 17, 20, 32
Computers, 12
Credit Reporting Agencies, 40
Credit Reports, 70
Creditors, 70
Department of Justice, 10, 77, 130
Dumpster Diving, 18
Electronic Funds Transfer Act, 55
Employers, 37, 42
Fair Credit Billing Act, 53, 56
False Identification, 49
FBI, 10, 14, 63, 87
Federal Trade Commission, 1, 23, 44, 52, 54, 62, 73, 77, 86, 128, 132
Freedom of Information Act, 14
Genealogy, 24
General Motors Corporation, 22
Hacking, 13
Identity Theft and Assumption Deterrence Act of 1998, 9, 125
INDEX, 109, 131
Information brokers, 14
Insider Access, 21
Internet, 11, 12, 13, 15, 23, 24, 33, 43, 64, 132
Internet Service Provider (ISP), 13
IRS, 46, 48
laws, 9, 83, 87, 125

Lexis-Nexis, 43
Liability, 55
Mail Theft, 16
Mastercard, 3
Motives, 6
Opt out, 30
Passwords, 39
Personal Identification Number (PIN), 21, 58
Personal Information, 76
Police Departments, 36
Pretexting, 25, 26

Privacy Act of 1974, 48
Privacy Rights Clearinghouse, 7, 28, 74, 77
P-Trak, 43
Secret Service, 3, 10, 63
Shoulder Surfing, 20
Skimmers, 24
Szwak, David, 5
Trans Union, 53
Trash Napping, 18
U.S. General Accounting Office, 3
Websites, 77

Notes

[1] U.S. Government Accounting Office, *Identity Theft: Information on Law Enforcement Efforts, Prevalence and Cost, Industry and Internet Issues,* May 1998.

[2] *Calls Soar to FTC's Identity Theft Hot Line,* APBNEWS.COM, July 12, 2000, http://www.apbnews.com/newscenter/breakingnews/

[3] Prepared statement of the Federal Trade Commission on Financial Identity Theft, April 22, 1999.

[4] Ibid.

[5] John Hanchette, *Identity Theft Tops List of Privacy Pirating,* Detroit News, April 26, 2000, Metro Section.

The Guide to Identity Theft Prevention

[6] Consumer Reports Online, www.consumerreports.com, *Are You a Target For Identity Theft?* September 1997.

[7] A CALPIRG/Privacy Rights Clearinghouse Report, *Nowhere to Turn: Victims Speak Out on Identity Theft,* May, 2000.

[8] Federal Trade Commission Identity Theft Hotline, http://www.consumer.gov/idtheft.

[9] R. O'Harrow and L. Leyden, *Firm Got Almost $1.5 Million in Federal Aid to Build Drivers License Database,* The Dallas Morning News, February 18, 1999, 6A.

[10] *Identity Thieves Plunder the Web,* www.apbnews.com, May 10, 2000.

[11] *Two Minutes and $14.95 for a Credit Report,* www.apbnews.com , May 10, 2000.

[12] Tom Arnold, *Internet Identity Theft: A Tragedy for Victims*, White Paper, June 2000.

[13] Department of the Treasury, U.S. Secret Service Testimony of Mr. James Bauer, Deputy Assistant Director, Office of Investigations, for presentation to the Subcommittee on Technology, Terrorism and Government Information of the Senate Judiciary Committee, May 20, 1990.

[14] Bill Lauterbach, *Danger on the Internet.*

[15] Cpl. Albert Jeffcoat, Coastal Empire Alliance Against Fraud, telephone interview, Feb. 13, 2001.

[16] The Los Angeles Times. *For Postal Thieves, Your Mailbox is a Mother Lode of Crime; All Those Numbers You Entrust to the Postal Service are Easy Pickings for Information-Age Crooks*, May 31, 2000.

[17] Newman, John Q., *Identity Theft: The Cybercrime of the Millennium,*

Loompanics Unlimited, 1999, p. 38.

[18] Mizell Jr., Louis R.. *Invasion of Privacy*. Berkley Publishing Group, 1998, p. 77.

[19] Los Angeles Times. *"Dumpster Diving" and Trashed Credit*, February 1, 1999.

[20] *Are You a Target for Identity Theft?*, Consumer Reports, Vol. 62, No. 9: Sept 1997, p. 11.

[21] The Detroit Free Press. *General Motors executives victims of credit card theft*. February 11, 2000.

[22] U.S. General Accounting Office, *Identity theft: Information on Prevalence, Cost and Internet Impact is Limited*, May, 1998.

[23] *Dateline NBC: Protecting Your Plastic*. NBC television broadcast, November 29, 1999.

[24] Federal Trade Commission. *Y2k Care: Protecting Your Finances from Year 2000 Scam Artists*, Consumer Alert, March 1999.

[25] Prepared statement of the Federal Trade Commission on Financial Identity Theft, April 22, 1999.

[26] Beth Schuster, *Gore Seeks Tougher Law Against Theft of Identity*, Los Angeles Times, June 8, 2000, B1.

[27] Cpl. Albert Jeffcoat, Coastal Empire Alliance Against Fraud, telephone interview, February 13, 2001.

[28] Traveler's Insurance Company Website. *Traveler's Property Casualty Provides Consumers with First Insurance Protection Against Identity theft Expenses*, http://www.travelers.com/idfraud.html.

[29] CALPIRG/ Privacy Rights Clearinghouse Report, *Nowhere to Turn: Victims Speak Out on Identity Theft,* May 2000; http://www.privacyrights.org/AR/idtheft2000.htm

[30] Social Security Administration. *Social Security: Your Number*, February 1998, http://www.ssa.gov

[31] Omaha World-Telegram, November 18, 1981, p.34 (Chicago Sun-Times News Service)

[32] Social Insecurity, http://www.msnbc.com/news/431520.asp

[33] Givens, Beth The Privacy Rights Handbook. Avon Books, 1997, p. 239

[34] Reiter, Luke, *Are You an Identity Theft Victim?*, available from http://www.zdnet.com/zdtv/cybercri...tures/story/0,3700,2104088,00.html

[35] Charrett, Sheldon, Identity, Privacy, and Personal Freedom: Big Brother vs. The New Resistance (Boulder, Colorado: Paladin Press, 1999)

[36] *Federal Trade Commission*, Identity Crisis…What to Do If Your Identity is Stolen (Consumer Alert, April 1999)

[37] Cpl. Albert Jeffcoat, Coastal Empire Alliance Against Fraud, telephone interview, February 13, 2001.

[38] FDIC Consumer News, Spring 1998, *A Crook Has Drained Your Account. Who Pays?*, http://www.fdic.gov/consumers/consumer/news/cnsprg98/crook.html

[39] Cpl. Albert Jeffcoat, Coastal Empire Alliance Against Fraud, telephone interview, February 13, 2001.

[40] Ibid.

[41] Goldman-Foley, Linda, Fact Sheet #17b, Identity Theft: Organizing Your Case, www.privacyrights.org

[42] Fact sheet#17: Coping with Identity Theft: What To Do When an

Johnny R. May

Imposter Strikes, www.privacyrights.org

[43] John Ingold, *"Thanks to Thieves, Checks No Longer in the Mail",* Denver Post, December 20, 2000. p. B-1

[44] *"Credit Card Scam at Vancouver Airport: Ripoff Operated from Improvement Booth",* The Edmonton Sun, November 19, 2000, p. 36

[45] Francine Latour, *Arrest Disrupts False ID, Title Ring Allegedly Used Registry Records",* The Boston Globe, December 13, 2000 , p. B1

[46] www.apbnews.com , FTC Chief Fell Prey to Credit Fraud, March 16, 2000.

[47] Margaret Mannix, *"Stolen Identity Can Ruin Your Credt- and That's Not the End,* U.S. News, June 1, 1998, www.usnews.com/usnews/issue/980601/1Thef.htm

[48] The Consumer X-Files, pp. 6-7

[49] Mark Larabee, *Identity Crime Fought Face-to-Face; Law Enforcement Agencies Joining Forces Against the Rising Crimes",* The Oregonian, September 21, 2000, p. E04

[50] Jan Faust, *Dealing with Identity Theft",* ABCNEWS.COM, October 9, 1998, http://abcnews.go.com/sections/us/DailyNews/id_theft981006 html

[51] Timothy O'Brien, *Identity Theft is Crime of Digital Era, Thanks to Net,* Seattle- PI.COM, wysiwyg://19/http://www.seattle-pi.com/national/iden03.shtml

[52] Rick Sarlat, *Police: Woman Stole ID to Pay for Childbirth,"* APBNEWS.COM, November 2, 2000, http://www.apbnews.com/newscenter/breakingnews/260/11/02/insurance1102_01.html

[53] M.L. Elrick, *13 Charged in Theft of Seniors' Names,* Detroit Free Press, October 17, 2000.

The Guide to Identity Theft Prevention

[54] Todd Venezia, *Police: Woman Had 350 Stolen Identities,* APBNEWS.COM, March 24, 2000, wysiwyg://58/http://www.apbnews.co...ews/2000/03/24/idtheft0324_0 1.html

[55] L.A. Johnson, *The Victim Had a Name to Die For.* Detroit Free Press, May 13, 1994.

[56] Frances Ann Burns, *Worker Accused of Stealing Cancer Patient Info*, APBNEWS.COM, August 8, 2000, http://www.apbnews.com/newscenter/breakingnews/2000/08/08/patient sc808_01.htm

[57] *Tiger Woods a Victim of Identity Theft*, APBNEWS.COM, December 19, 2000, http://www.apb.com/newscenter/breakingnews/.../tiger1219_01.htm

[58] *Morgue Workers Accused of Stealing from Dead*, APBNEWS.COM, December 20, 2000, http://www.apb.com/newscenter/breakingnews/morgue1220_01.htm

About the Author

Johnny R. May, CPP, CPO is an independent security consultant and trainer who specializes in protecting people from identity theft. He is currently employed by Henry Ford Community College in Dearborn, Michigan, where he serves as a crime prevention specialist with the college's campus safety department.

Mr. May has lectured extensively on security and crime prevention topics and is regularly cited by the media as a leading authority.

A graduate of the University of Detroit-Mercy, Mr. May earned his B.S. in Criminal Justice and his M.S in Security Administration. He is an adjunct professor at the University of Detroit -Mercy, Madonna University, and Henry Ford Community College. He has also been designated as a Certified Protection Professional (CPP) by the American Society for Industrial Security, and as a Certified Protection Officer (CPO) by the International Foundation for Protection Officers. He is a member of The International Society of Crime Prevention Practitioners (ISCPP) and the American Society for Industrial Security (ASIS). He serves on the Executive Board for the Detroit Chapter of ASIS and is a member of the organization's Standing Committee on Academic Programs in Colleges and Universities.

To contact the author call (248)745-6221
or email at SECRES@prodigy.net

NOTES

NOTES

NOTES

Printed in the United States
4211